OUR
AMERICAN
TREES

BY THE AUTHOR

SEA SHELLS

OUR AMERICAN TREES

OUR AMERICAN TREES

BY

RUTH H. DUDLEY

ILLUSTRATED BY

NILS HOGNER

THOMAS Y. CROWELL COMPANY

NEW YORK

The author wishes to thank the United States Forest Service—particularly Mr. Woodbridge Metcalf, Extension Forester, University of California—and Mr. Robert L. Crowell, for their helpful suggestions in preparing this book.

The illustrator wishes to extend thanks to Mr. E. J. Alexander, Associate Curator, New York Botanical Garden, for his assistance in the research for the drawings.

PROPERTY OF
CIPOLE SCHOOL DIST. #45

269

Copyright © 1956 by Ruth H. Dudley
All rights reserved. No part of this book may be reproduced in any form, except by a reviewer, without the permission of the publisher.
Manufactured in the United States of America
LIBRARY OF CONGRESS CATALOG CARD NO. 56-9800
1 2 3 4 5 6 7 8 9 10

To Mother and "Panny"

who have shared with me many happy hours camping among the trees. And to all my readers, young and old, I dedicate this book in the hope it may add some small bit to the growing awareness in our land of the importance of trees.

CONTENTS

1	OUR FORESTS WHEN THE PILGRIMS ARRIVED	1
2	HOW A TREE GROWS	10
3	JUST GROWING	23
4	OUR FORESTS TODAY	27
5	MAKING OUR BARREN LANDS GREEN	42
6	SOFTWOOD TREES THAT GIVE US LUMBER	48
7	HARDWOOD TREES THAT GIVE US LUMBER	57
8	TREES THAT GIVE US FUEL	68
9	TREES THAT GIVE US PAPER	74
10	TREES THAT GIVE US CLOTH	80
11	TREES THAT GIVE US CHEMICALS	84
12	TREES THAT GIVE US FOOD	90
13	OUR BIGGEST TREES	97

14	OUR SMALLEST TREES	108
15	OUR RAREST TREES	115
16	OUR MOST PLENTIFUL TREES	124
17	THINGS YOU CAN DO	130
	BOOKS ABOUT TREES	141
	INDEX	143

OUR AMERICAN TREES

1

OUR FORESTS WHEN THE PILGRIMS ARRIVED

THINK of how America looked when the Pilgrims landed on our shores. Trees! Nothing but trees! Everywhere, as far as the eye could see, were towering forests.

Had we been pioneers then we surely would have been as amazed as they. All along our Atlantic coast, wherever our forefathers landed, it was the same. Trees right down to the water's edge. Trees stretching away and away into the distance. More trees than they had seen in a lifetime before. They must have thought America just one great, thick forest!

As the years went by, their children and grandchildren must have thought so, too. For though the pioneers pushed farther and farther west, still they found forests. Not until over a hundred years later did the pioneers come to the Mississippi Valley and the open prairie. Surely now, they must have thought, we are through the forests at last. They must have been even more certain of this when, hundreds of miles farther west, they came to the treeless Great Plains.

But the pioneers had another surprise in store. They pushed along the Plains and came finally to the Rocky Mountains. And there before their astonished eyes—more trees! Stretching away and away, towering up and up, were our great Western forests.

Actually nearly one half of America's great lands were forests when the Pilgrims arrived. About nine hundred million acres of land were blessed with forests. From east to west, from north to south across America stretched forests. Only the wide central plains were treeless.

Everywhere the Pilgrims looked were thick woods and towering trees. And they did not like it. Certainly they did not think these trees a blessing. Had we been with them then we might not have thought so either.

Such thick, far-reaching woods had not been in their plans at all. Clear meadows and fields were what they had in mind. Fine stretches of land to cultivate. Room for their crops and their homes.

At home in Europe they had become used to neat

fields and hedges. These huge trees seemed to tower over and around them like enemies. The one great desire of the settlers was to clear their land of the "terrible trees." So they chopped, burned, and hacked away to make room for cabins, gardens, and fields.

Turning forests into cleared land wasn't easy to do. It was hard, slow work cutting down these big trees with an ax. It was dangerous, too, and many a man was crippled or killed by falling limbs and trees.

Often a settler found cutting or burning too slow. Eager to get in his crops, he learned from the Indians to girdle the trees. By hacking out circlets of bark around the trunks, a grove of trees could be quickly killed. This was called "deadening." The trees, though still standing, were dead, so enough sunlight came through the leafless remains for the settler to raise his crops. He found this a poor method in the long run, however. When storms set in, dead limbs and whole trees came crashing down across his land.

At first the pioneers thought only of getting the trees out of their way. Later they began cutting the trees for the wood and the millions of things needed to build civilization—homes, stores, bridges, bobsleds, even shingles and matches.

More and more settlers came over. More and more

forests were cleared for farms. More lumber was needed to build homes and towns. There were no sawmills at first, so whole tree trunks were used to build the cabins. One trunk was piled on another, often with the bark left on. Using whole trees this way, it took a great many just to build the log cabin homes, barns, and stockades. Vast numbers of trees were cut and burned to clear the land for towns and roads.

Many of the trees that grew in these New England forests were beautiful white pine. The colonists found the wood of these white pines soft and light and strong. And it was easy to work with.

Great Britain discovered this, too. The white pines were great, handsome trees in those early days. Some towered up as high as two hundred fifty feet. And there was a good eighty feet of straight solid trunk before the branches began. These trunks made wonderful masts for the British ships—and England needed them badly. Nowhere else could the British find trees like that. Men were sent into our white pine forests to mark the tallest and stoutest of these trees, to be set aside for the British Navy.

The American colonists were told not to touch the trees that carried this British mark. The colonists did not like to be ordered about this way. They

wanted these fine white pines for themselves. This led to trouble between England and America. It helped bring about the Revolutionary War.

These early white pine forests were the greatest forests America has known. And wood from these white pines was the finest wood ever used. In those days nothing was known about conservation. No one thought about saving or replanting trees. Had we been living then we probably would not have thought about it either. No one dreamed those miles of forests could ever be used up with so few people here and such great stretching lands.

But as more and more settlers came, great sawmills were built and more and more trees came crashing to the earth. The fame of our white pines spread to other countries—countries where such strong, soft wood was unknown. White pine became a valuable export. It was shipped to many distant ports. Many early Americans made great fortunes cutting down these forests and selling white pine wood.

This went on through the years until many miles of our land lay open and barren. People then knew little about careful cutting. They took only the very best parts of the trees, leaving the rest to rot. This was wasteful and dangerous. Fires started easily. And the wood left to rot fed the flames until they roared across mile after mile of woodland destroying still more forests and wild life—and people.

In 1871 a great fire started in the cut-over forest near Peshtigo, Wisconsin. The "Peshtigo Horror" it was later called. This terrible fire killed over eleven hundred people and destroyed miles of forests and everything in them—homesteads, domestic animals, and wildlife. In those days the pioneers had no way to fight forest fires as we have now. Once started, the fires had to be left to burn themselves out.

Things like this went on year after year. Finally a few people began to worry about the way our forests were being destroyed. They tried to have laws passed to save the trees. But most of the people did not understand. They had come to America to be free. Why couldn't they do as they wished?

Perhaps we would have felt the same way, too, had we been living then. For they had not yet learned the true meaning of liberty. They thought liberty meant freedom to do as they wished, without thought of another; without thought of the good of the country or the people as a whole; without thought of future generations.

And so vast acres of forests—in the East, the Middle West, and the South—were cut and hauled away. Until finally they came to the last frontier in the West.

It was a sad thing for America to lose those virgin forests—especially the great white pines. For it was the white pine, more than any other tree, that built America in our country's first three hundred years. But in doing so this tree was destroyed.

It is said that if you cut into a sash or door from an old New England house, even today, you will find beautiful white pine wood from trees that were growing (probably in Maine) during the Revolution. In New England, whole villages built of white pine are still standing, but today there are few white pines in the region suitable for first-grade lumber.

Never again will we see those trees as they once stood, thick and towering and beautiful. True, they are growing again now in the East—but not, of course, as they once were.

As the pioneers moved across the country they left great stretches of barren ground where thick forests once stood. Then storms began to bring floods. On barren mountainsides there were no longer any trees to hold back the rainfall. Water rushed down. It cut deep gullies and caused floods in the rivers and lowlands.

When people saw what was happening they began to understand better how important our forests were. They realized that our forests were not endless. Nor could they be grown again, like grain, in one season, or ten.

Finally, in 1905, Congress passed the law that started our Forest Service. At first the Forest Service men were kept busy just trying to protect the woods we had left from damage by fire and mankind. It was slow work. And it was very discouraging. Too many people still did not understand, or did not want to understand. Even Congress was not interested enough to vote the Forest Service the money it needed to carry on as it should.

It took a terrible happening to arouse the country.

WHEN THE PILGRIMS ARRIVED

One very dry summer, in 1910, thousands of fires broke out through the Idaho forests. Gale winds at seventy miles an hour swept through the trees. They sent the scorching flames racing across hundreds of miles of beautiful forest land. Acres of rotting lumber, left by careless cutting, fed the roaring fires. The small Forest Service was helpless. Whole towns went up in smoke. For weeks the fires raged on, until rain put the flames out at last.

A sickening sight met the people's eyes—ashes, knee deep, where mile after mile green forests had stood. An area about as big as the state of Connecticut was completely burned over.

It roused the country to action. At last the Forest Service was given help to do the tremendous job that lay ahead. Since that time a great deal has been learned about replanting trees and taking care of our forests.

2

HOW A TREE GROWS

STRANGE as it may seem, trees are not so different from us. Stand one of your friends beside a tree. Chances are you won't see anything alike about them at all. Except, of course, that they both are alive and standing.

But they are very much alike, really. The more we look into the wondrous ways of a tree, the more we see how much they have in common with us.

We must breathe to stay alive—so must a tree. It is breathing constantly day and night.

We have skin for protection; a tree has bark over its trunk and branches. And a leaf has an outer skin to protect its inner, vital parts.

We have a spinal column; a tree has sturdy heartwood.

We have human flesh; a tree has wood tissue, busy with hundreds of hard-working cells.

HOW A TREE GROWS

We have red corpuscles in our bodies; the leaves of a tree have tiny green dots. These are the real "hard workers" of the tree and they look very much like our red corpuscles.

We rest at night—so does a tree.

We are born with a strong urge to live and to reproduce our kind. A tree seems to have this, too.

We have our troubles—so does a tree. Heat and cold, pests and disease, for instance. And the thoughtless cruelty of mankind. Often a tree fights fiercely for life against great odds.

We must eat to keep alive—so must a tree.

Perhaps you have heard the expression, "He lives on wind and air sauce!" It's usually said of a person who doesn't seem to eat very much. At first glance it would seem a tree is rather that way, for it lives on nothing but water, air, and sunshine. But there is really much more to it than that.

A tree does have good nourishing food, which it makes itself. Not out of "wind and air sauce" exactly. But out of water, air, and sunshine.

In doing this a tree is much "smarter" than we are. When we're hungry we have to go out and get our food. Perhaps we buy it at a restaurant or grocery store, or we may gather it from our gardens. Hundreds of man-hours of work are needed to give you just a hamburger and a milk shake. Great industries are busy with the growing and preparing and selling of foods. Millions of people are giving hours upon hours of labor.

And a tree? All it does is stand still. And working quietly, out of water from its roots, out of air, it manufactures all the food it needs. It feeds itself—and all the world, you might say. For if it weren't for this secret process known only to green plants and trees you would not be here today. No one of us would be living on this earth!

If trees and plants could not feed themselves they could not exist. And if they did not exist no animals could live, including mankind. This process of manufacturing food is called *photosynthesis*. And it is so amazing that even our most brilliant scientists do not as yet understand exactly how it is done. It is one of the most important things in our whole living earth.

Of course, in order to carry on this food-making business, the trees must have certain "tools" with which to work. And it is work, though not easy-to-see work like plowing a field or gathering grain.

Sunlight is one of the "tools" a tree must have for its food making. It's the fuel the leaves use to keep the factory running. That is why the leaves grow on the trees the way they do, so they can catch and hold as much sunlight as possible. At night, of course, trees rest. But all day long, from sunrise to sunset, working a day shift only, the trees busily carry on their magic.

Inside the protective layer of "skin," each leaf has tiny bundles of matter. These are called *chloroplasts*, and they look like green dots. Scientists find they are rather like our own red corpuscles. And the *chlorophyll* they give to the leaf is quite similar, in substance, to our own blood.

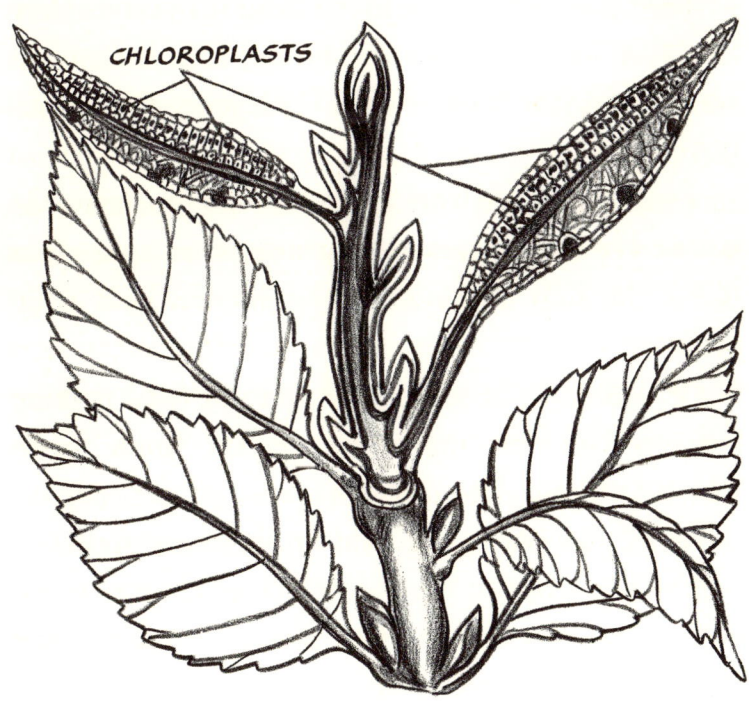

It is the work of these tiny green dots that seems so amazing to us. For out of the air and water they make sugar. In the "skin" covering of the leaf there are many tiny holes or pores. These holes are called *stomata* and are used in breathing. Through its holes the leaf breathes in oxygen from the air and gives off carbon dioxide. It must do this to keep alive, just as we must.

But, strangely enough—and even more important—it also breathes in carbon dioxide and gives off oxygen. Carbon dioxide is poison to us. It's a waste product given off by all living things. But a leaf can take this "poison" from the air and turn it into carbohydrates, the basic food of all plant and animal life.

To help in this work, water is sent up from the roots. This water comes up through tiny pipelines in the trunk. It travels along the branches and twigs and into the veins of the leaves. The tiny green dots in the leaf use the sun in some secret way to turn this water and the carbon dioxide into food. Scientists cannot do it. But a tree can.

Sugar is made first. Perhaps it's the easiest to make. Anyway, we know sugar dissolves quickly in water and gives quick energy. That is why we often take chocolate bars on our hikes.

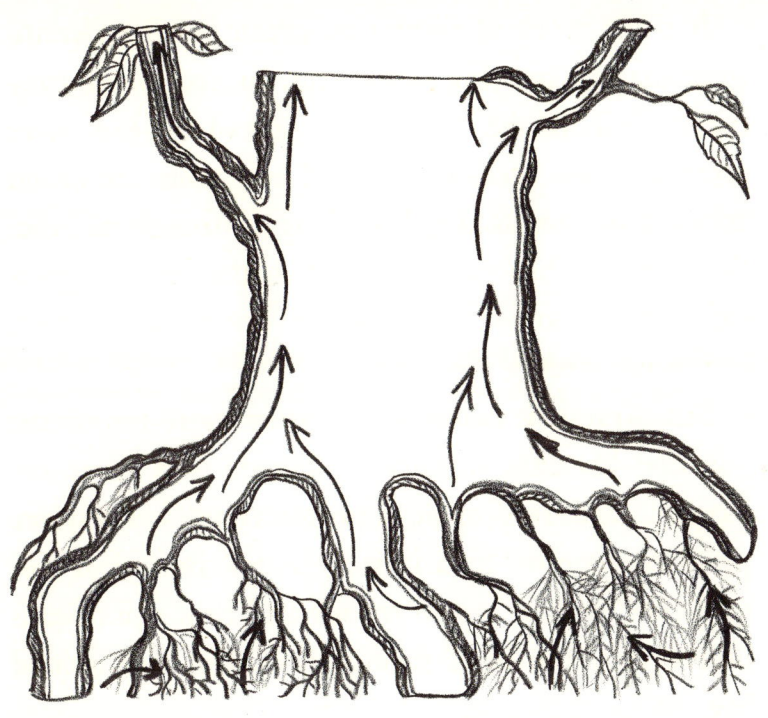

A tree, too, can use sugar quickly and easily. And it does, sending the sugar to all its growing parts. But a tree cannot live on sugar alone, any more than we can. It uses what sugar it needs. Then it turns the rest into starch and other foods, such as proteins, oil, and cellulose.

This process, too, is an amazing one. But the tree goes about it in its own busy, secret way. Scientists tell us that it takes a thousand square feet of leaf surface to make about one pound of starch during five hours of bright sunlight.

A tree cannot digest this starch, but makes it only to store. The starch is sent down into all parts of the tree to be tucked away in roots, branches, trunks, and leaves for future use. The tree cannot carry on its food making at night or during periods of cold. So it must have an extra supply in store for just such times.

When needed, this starch is sent back up to the leaves. The leaves once again use their magic. They turn the starch back into sugar and other necessary foods. These foods flow into all the growing parts of the tree in the form of sap. It's this sugary sap that is taken from the maple trees when they are tapped in the spring and made into the maple syrup you use on your pancakes. Since the mature tree produces more sap than it needs, it is possible to drain off some of this sugary solution with little or no damage to the tree's life process. A tree fifteen inches thick, for instance, would lose only about seven per cent of its stored sugar.

The roots of a tree have two important jobs to do. They anchor the tree firmly in the earth so winds will not topple it over. And they collect water to send up to the leaves.

Some trees have roots that do a fine anchoring

job. Roots of an oak, for instance, go deep into the earth and hold the tree so firmly that the strongest gale isn't likely to blow it down. Other trees, like the maple and spruce, have only surface roots. It is harder for them to withstand a really bad windstorm.

Roots spread out, too, over a very large area. Generally you can say the spread of a tree's roots is as great as the spread of its branches.

Roots branch off and divide, the divisions becoming smaller until at the end they're tiny hairs. But tiny though they are, they have important work to do. It's the younger, smaller roots that soak up water and minerals from the soil. Under a big tree there'll be millions of these tiny, hairlike roots spread out below ground. And they'll all be busily soaking up moisture with their very absorbent "skin."

Scientists say that if all the roots under one big oak could be stretched out in one straight line, the line would reach for several hundred miles.

After a while, of course, the younger roots grow older and toughen. Then they no longer soak up moisture from the soil. Instead they serve as channels to carry water from the younger roots into the tree trunk. And, of course, they help anchor the tree to the ground.

At the growing tip of each root is a little caplike covering. This cap acts like a sensitive "feeler." Somehow it is able to "feel" rocks or anything in its way and work around them, guiding the root growth into safer paths. Some scientists call these mysterious root tips guiding "brains."

Next time you're enjoying the shade of a widespreading tree, you might think of its marvelous root system which you cannot even see. When you admire the cool green leaves above, remember the workers below—those millions of tiny, hairlike roots busily growing and soaking up water so the leaves can be cool and green and you can have this blessed shade.

A tree trunk has important work to do, too. The illustration of a trunk's cross section will show you all its parts. The tough outer layer of bark protects the next softer inner layer of bark. This inner bark does need protection, for running through it are many long tubes, or pipelines. Through these passes the food the leaves have made and sent back down.

There is a second set of tubes, or pipelines, farther inside the tree. These carry the water from the roots to the leaves.

The main growing part of the tree is the section between these two sets of tubes. It is called the *cambium layer*. Here very active and very important cells are busily at work, growing both fore and aft.

On the inner side the cells are making new pipelines to carry the food. This new, soft, moist layer is called *sapwood*. As new pipelines are built each year, the old ones slowly dry up. They harden and become the dead center of the trunk, or *heartwood*. This heartwood really is dead, for it no longer plays

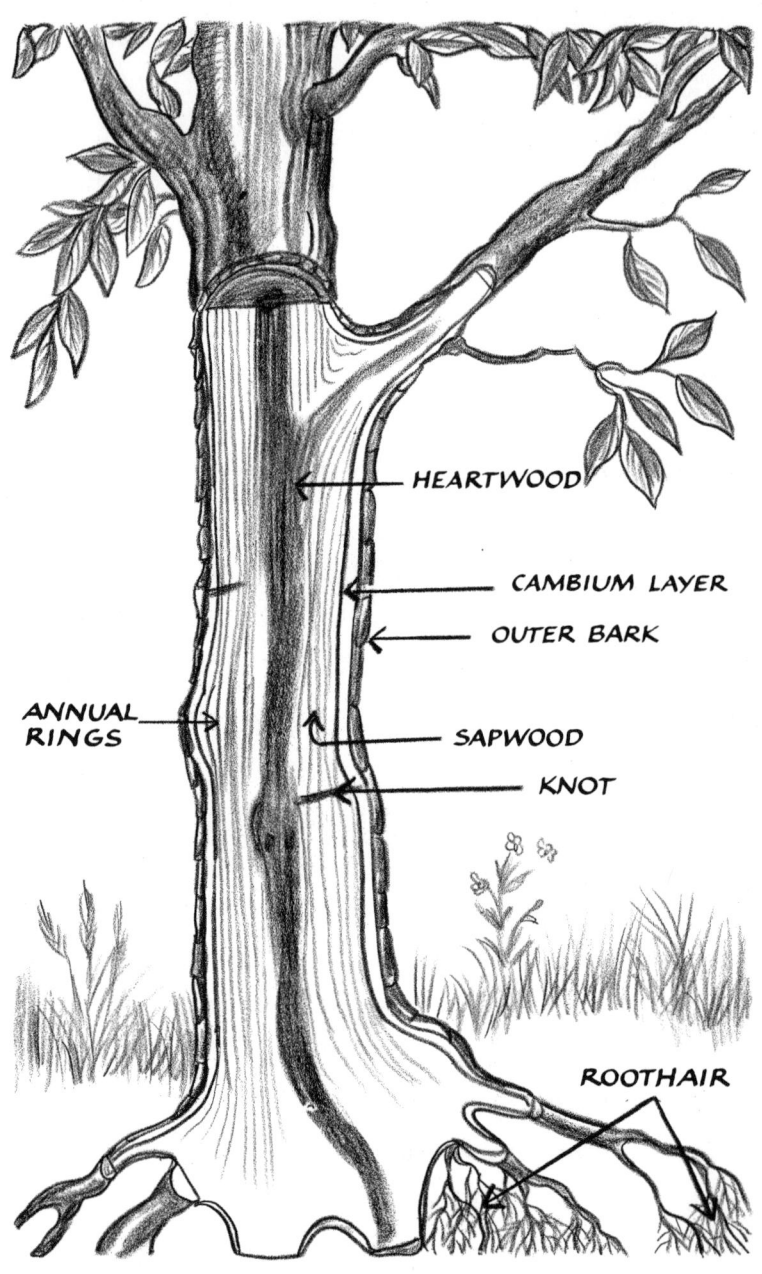

any active part in the work going on inside the tree. And since most of the trunk is heartwood you can see that the greater part of any tree trunk isn't even alive. Only a very small part does all the active work.

Trees with their heartwood completely destroyed by fire or disease can go on living. Perhaps you've seen trees like that in the forest, still alive and green. But they aren't as strong as they once were. They need this solid, inner wood—this "spinal column"—to give them strength to stand against storm winds.

On the outer side of the cambium layer the cells are making fresh inner bark—a new layer each year. The new layers of bark aren't easy to see. But the rings of wood are quite noticeable in any cross section of trunk. And if you count these rings you usually can tell how old the tree is. Generally one new ring is formed each year. The old layers turn slowly into outer bark.

A tree grows larger around only on the surface. That is, growth in the width of a tree takes place only in its thin cambium layers—the inner bark and sapwood. This yearly new growth keeps pushing against the old bark. If the outer bark can't stretch enough to make room for this new growth, it splits and tears. That's what makes the deep furrows you see in some tree trunks. It is also why strips of old bark peel off on some trees like the sycamore and birch, or hang loose as on the shagbark and hickory.

A tree grows taller in an unusual way, too. It grows taller only at the top. A branch six feet from the ground will never be any higher, no matter how tall the tree grows. If a limb on your favorite back yard tree is just right this year for climbing, it will always be that way as long as it stays on the tree. The limb will grow longer and larger around. But it will never grow any higher from the ground than it is right now.

A tree lengthens out from the top or the outer ends of its branches. Branches at the top bud out into new branches. And side branches grow out from side buds.

You can watch this happen if you cut a few twigs or small branches from a tree and put them in water. In a few weeks you will see that the end bud bursts open and grows out into a twig. New side sections will eventually lengthen out from side buds.

In this same way a tree grows taller.

3

JUST GROWING

Just by growing, trees are important.

We have seen how the leaves take in carbon dioxide, which is poison to us, and give off oxygen. This oxygen helps to purify the air we breathe—a good thing for us and for all animal life.

Trees can make quite a difference in our climate. While the leaves are working they are constantly giving off moisture. The roots send up more water than the leaves can use. The rest is sprayed out into the air through their tiny pores or stomata. In fact, scientists have found that a good-sized willow can give off as much as five thousand gallons of water during a hot summer day!

This water is in the form of vapor so, of course, we don't notice it. Any more than we notice our lungs giving off moisture when we breathe—except on cold winter days, when we say we can "see our breath." This moisture given off by the trees is important to all growing things. It keeps the woods and forests cool and moist. It spreads out into all the countryside around so that it even affects the temperature. If you have ever slipped gratefully from a scorching hot field into a cool green woods on a very hot day you know how true this is.

Oceans send up moisture for the clouds to carry and drop as rain over the land. But all the rains that drop on land are not from "ocean clouds." There are "tree clouds" that drop a good part of the rain, and these are every bit as important.

If one willow will give off as much as five thousand gallons in one day, think of the huge amount of vapor a forest of trees will give off. This vapor rises toward the sky. It cools the air and adds moisture to the clouds.

Winds carry this forest moisture great distances inland where rain is needed. Much of the moisture that falls in our interior states is from "tree clouds," not "ocean clouds." This is because "ocean clouds" (clouds formed by evaporation from the ocean) cannot get over the high mountain ranges along the way. The cold mountain air condenses the vapor and it falls as rain before it can get to our inland prairie states.

JUST GROWING

Prairie lands beyond the mountain ranges would be in a bad way if they had to depend on "ocean clouds." So the "tree clouds," are very necessary.

Forests play an important part, too, in holding onto the water once it has fallen as rain. The leaves, twigs, and branches of the trees break the fall of the rain and snow. The water reaches the ground more slowly, dripping instead of pouring. When it does reach the ground, there is much forest material beneath the trees to soak it up. The dead leaves and twigs make a thick forest carpet. This acts like a great sponge. As much as forty-six tons of water can be soaked up by one acre of forest carpet. The water held back in this way seeps out gradually into our streams and rivers, keeping them clean and well filled for our use. It even helps the fish life, too. The next time you carry home a fine string of fish, remember that the trees helped you get them!

Scientists say that nearly three billion tons of our topsoil are washed or blown away each year because of treeless places. Where forests have been cut or burned, there is nothing to hold back the water. A pelting downpour can send down a hillside as much as four hundred tons of water for every acre! This water is caught and held and turned to good use if the hillside is covered with trees. But on a bare hillside the pouring rain cuts deep gullies. The water and earth rushing down together cause great damage. Lands and rivers below are flooded and filled with silt. You probably have read about, or perhaps seen, some of the terrible floods in our country, and in other countries, too. If the forests had not been destroyed these floods would not have happened.

Tree roots help hold our soil. They prevent the wind from blowing it away. We know, for instance, how far and wide the roots of one big oak tree can reach. One hundred such trees growing in a five-mile area can form three or four miles of strong root-cords to help hold our soil.

Since the tree roots soak up so much moisture, they are useful for draining swamplands where mosquitoes breed. In some places trees are being planted to do just this.

It is obvious why trees are important to our bird life, too. Every part of nature is perfectly balanced. We need our birds and wild life as well as our trees. Each has its own special part to play. When any one part of nature is destroyed, all the other parts suffer. And, of course, so does mankind.

More and more we are coming to realize that trees, aside from the products they give us, are very important just growing.

4

OUR FORESTS TODAY

The thick forests and towering trees the pioneers knew are gone, it's true. But we still have forests. In fact, stretching across America, there are six different kinds of forests. And many different kinds of trees make up these forests.

Some trees, like the white pine, do better where it is cold; some, like the palm, need warmth. Some trees need lots of rain and dampness; others get along with much less. Some trees like high mountain country. Other trees like the lowlands and valleys. So in different parts of our country where climate and growing conditions differ, we find different kinds of trees.

There are some trees that thrive in most any kind of climate—just as some people can. These trees we find growing in many parts of our country. For instance, if you lived in Maine you might have a pretty aspen growing on your front lawn. And if you had a cousin living clear across the country in California he, too, might have an aspen on his front lawn. This tree can grow almost anywhere.

Trees, wherever they grow, fall into two main family groups—*conifers* and *broadleafs*. A conifer is a cone-bearing tree and bears its seeds in cones. The seeds are attached to the underside of the cone scales, and each seed has a wing. When the cones are ripe, the scales separate and the seeds fall out and fly away on the wind. The seeds that land on fertile ground take root, and new conifers are started.

A broadleaf tree reproduces itself in a different way. Seeds in the broadleaf family develop in the flowers. The seeds are the tree's fruit, and different broadleaf trees develop this fruit in different ways. The apple blossom, for example, develops into the apple fruit with its seeds protected by the flesh of the apple. The pecan nut meat is the seed, or fruit, of the pecan tree and is protected on the tree by the outer husk and hard inner shell.

Seeds of the holly and dogwood trees are hidden inside their berry fruit. And the acorn is the seed produced by the oak. When the different kinds of fruit of the broadleafs ripen, the seeds are scattered—

by birds, animals, wind, and people—and new trees spring up.

A conifer is more commonly called a needle tree (because of its needlelike leaves) or a softwood (because the wood of most conifers is soft). Most softwoods are evergreen. Their leaves, or needles, stay on through the year.

Trees in the broadleaf family are commonly called leaf trees. Their leaves are broader than the needle-leaves of the conifers. The maple leaf, for instance, is much broader than the pine needle. Broadleaf trees are also called *hardwoods*, because their wood is usually hard.

Most of the hardwoods are not evergreen (except those growing in warmer sections). Their leaves do not stay on all year. Because of this they are called by still another name—deciduous trees.

Some forests are made up mostly of softwoods; other forests have many more hardwood trees. And in still others the softwoods and hardwoods grow side by side.

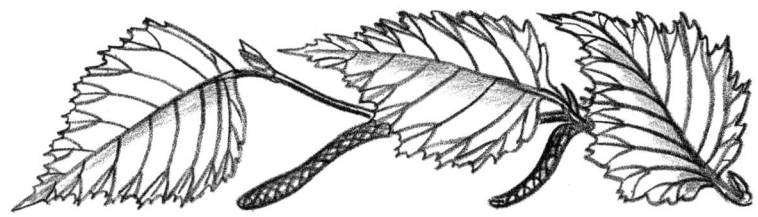

The Northern Forest

The northern forest takes in our New England and Great Lakes states. The softwoods are the main trees here. They like the long, cold winters and rather short summers of this northern region. Here you find spruces, balsam, firs, larch, and several kinds of pines. This is the forest where the white pine was so important. There are some hardwood trees here, too, such as maples, birches, and aspens.

Because the pioneers settled in this part of the country, this great northern forest was the first to be wastefully used by the early settlers and lumbermen. All across this northern forest the trees were cut and burned. Six-sevenths of the state of Wisconsin, for instance, was once covered with pines and hemlocks, but none of this original forest is left.

Trees came back on these devastated lands, it is true—but not the valuable timber trees. Instead, quick-growing trees such as firs, spruces, and aspen took over and now cover about one third of this forest area. But these are not good timber trees. They are used mainly for pulpwood and fuel. So the problem is how to get better trees growing again on these lands that once were thick woods, where now mostly brambles and firewood and "weed trees" grow.

OUR FORESTS TODAY

"Weed trees" are so called because they are not of much value commercially. But we must not frown on any tree. Even "weed trees" are growing trees and are important as such. They lend beauty to the land, food and shelter to the wild life, and they hold down the soil. Besides, every year our scientists are finding new uses for various kinds of wood. Any day these "weed trees" might become important commercially, as hemlock did in the manufacture of rayon, cellophane, and plastics (see chapter X).

Meanwhile, thanks to our Forest Service, we are slowly repairing the sorry damage done to our original great forests. White pine has been replanted on some of the land in the northern forest. It is not as towering a tree as it once was—it would take many years to grow that huge again. But "second growth" white pines are becoming important again.

Red pine, too, is coming back. It grew thick in the early forests, but it was destroyed by settlers. Since red pine is quick growing and hardy, it's a fine tree to use in replanting.

OUR AMERICAN TREES

The Hardwood or Deciduous Forest

The hardwood forest, or deciduous forest, is in the central part of the eastern half of our country. Here, as you can tell by the name, the hardwood trees are the most important. They like the milder winters and the longer summers of this region. And the soil suits them, too.

In this forest once grew great stretches of maples, birches, and beeches. Dense beech forests alone covered a great part of Ohio, Kentucky, Indiana, and central Michigan. Elms, ashes, and oaks were thick here, as were lindens and hickories, tulip trees and sweet gum. There were softwoods, too, such as pine and hemlock.

Our beautiful, now rare, black walnut once grew so thickly the pioneers used its wood for everything from rail fences to cradles and gunstocks. Its hard wood does not float when green as does soft wood, so the colonists could not transport it. Instead they used it for anything at hand.

Now these handsome black walnut trees are hard to find. The best ones grow in the southern Appalachians.

In spite of the ravages of fire and the wastefulness of settlers, this still is the largest region of hardwood

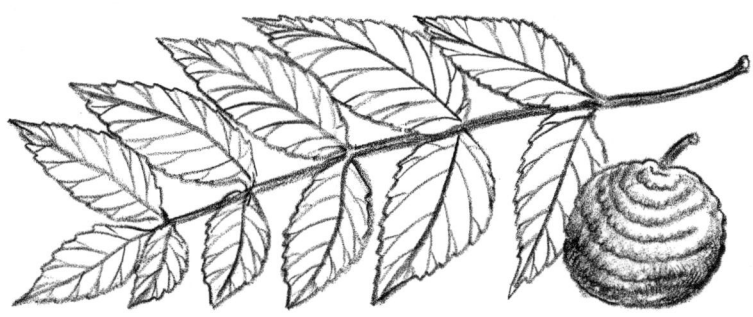

trees in our country. Most of the same trees grow here as grew in early times, but in smaller quantities. However, we finally have learned the value of our trees, and replanting and proper cutting is being carried out in much of this area. We are working to reforest these lands again.

The Southern Forest

The southern forest runs through the southeastern and Gulf states from North Carolina to Texas. Softwood trees grow best in this region. In early days the white pine was the most important tree in this forest, too. It grew thick and tall along the southern Appalachians. When the white pines in the northern forest had been used up, lumbermen took these, then the southern yellow pines.

Over one hundred and fifty million acres of southern pines were cut over and burned. Fortunately a great deal of this has come back as second growth trees. Even land that once grew cotton has been replanted in pine; you can still see traces of the furrows among the trees that are being lumbered.

Southern pines now furnish some of our very best softwood lumber. In fact, they are the only important source of large timber in the eastern half of the United States. They also give us rosin and turpentine, as well as lumber and pulpwood. Some fine hardwood trees grow in this region, too—trees such as magnolia, ash, sweet gum, oak, cypress, and tupelo.

The Rocky Mountain Forest

The Rocky Mountain forest reaches from Canada to Mexico. It stretches in a slanting line across our country in the Rocky Mountains. The forests in this region are scattered. In between the small forest sections are many large, bare areas where no trees grow.

Hardwoods such as oaks, aspens, cottonwoods, and sycamores grow in these forests. But most of the trees are softwoods—pines, spruces, firs. However, they are not the same species as those in the northeastern states. The main growth here is the western white pine, ponderosa pine, lodgepole pine, Douglas fir, and Englemann's spruce.

TURPENTINE WORKER

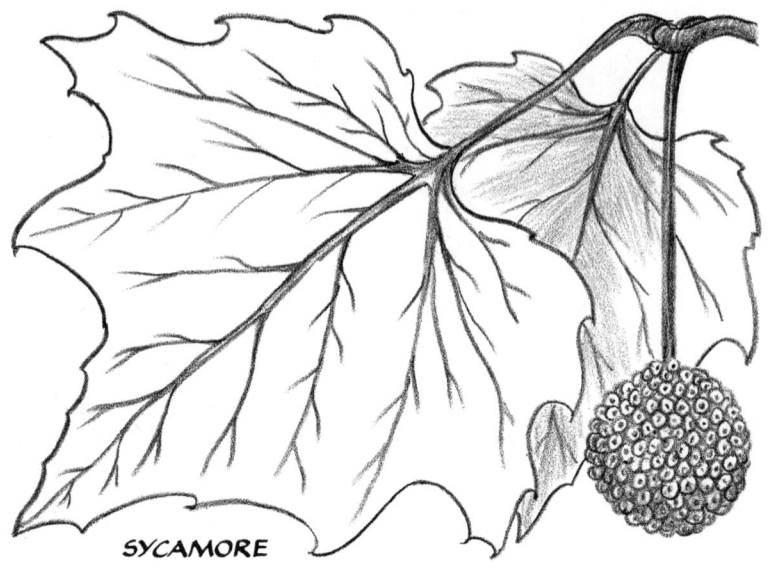

SYCAMORE

At one time these great trees stretched for miles and miles across this Rocky Mountain region. That was before the early lumbermen arrived. After the eastern forests were used up and middle west and southern forests were depleted, the lumbermen moved west. The western white pine was especially in demand. It was almost as fine as the eastern white pine once had been.

It was in this region, in Idaho, that the great fires in 1910 showed the people at last the horror that could be caused by careless cutting. Today a second growth of western white pines covers many parts of this burned area. Replanting is being carried on in here, too.

OUR FORESTS TODAY

The Pacific Coast Forest

The Pacific Coast forest is our westernmost forest area. Both softwoods and hardwoods grow thickly here. Fortunately the Forest Service was started in time to save this area from the fate of our eastern forests, so trees that are centuries old still stand in parts of this region.

Most of the species are different from those of the eastern woods. The most important trees here are the Douglas fir, pines, and redwoods.

It is a rather small forest area. In fact, three-fourths of our forests today are east of the plains states. And most of them are east of the Mississippi River. The Pacific forest covers only about one-seventh of the whole forest area of the United States. But it is very important to our lumber industry. It contains more than one-half of our total saw timber—trees that give us big timber.

Virgin forests are forests in which no lumbering has been done. Today seven-eighths of our original virgin forests are gone.

Of these grand old trees, only the Douglas fir is left. And this is found only in a small area—about fifty miles—between the Cascade Mountains and the Pacific Ocean.

MANGROVE

The Tropical Forest

The tropical forest in this country is a very small area in southern Florida and Texas. In this forest you find trees that usually grow only in the tropics, trees such as the palms, mangrove, beefwood, and mahogany.

Some of these trees were brought over and planted by man. Others started from seeds brought over by birds or from seeds that were washed ashore by the waves.

The bald cypress and live oak are interesting trees here. They are not purely tropical, however, and they also grow farther north.

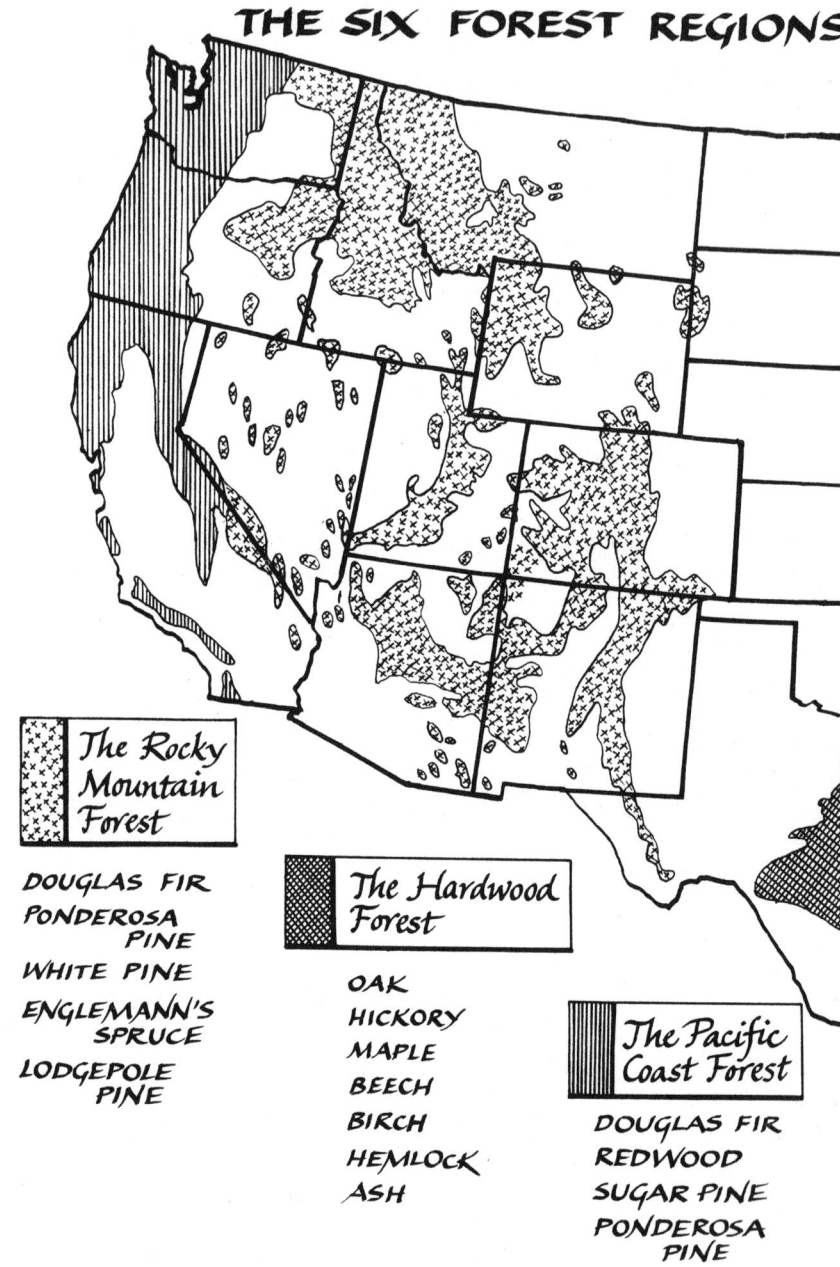

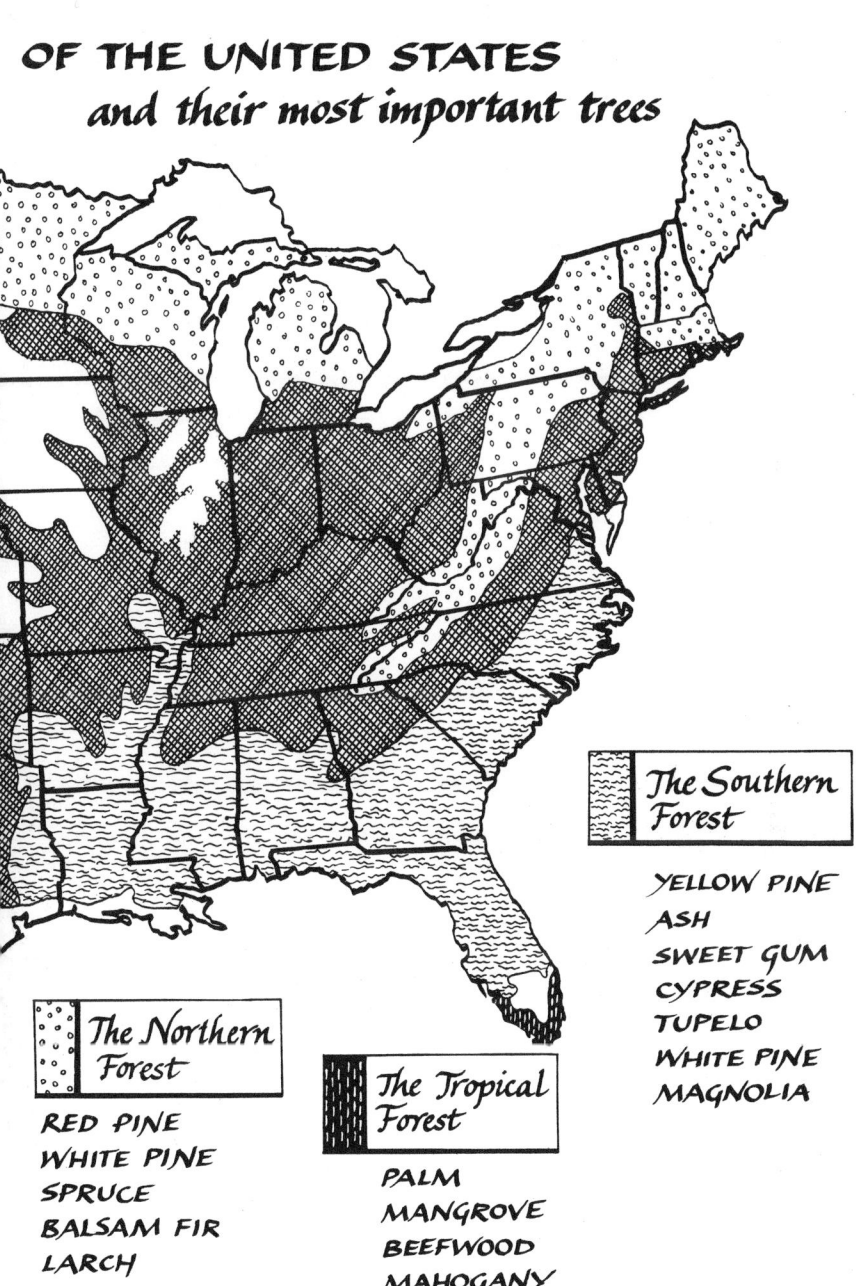

5

MAKING OUR BARREN LANDS GREEN

WE know now that our trees and our forest lands are among our most precious possessions. In all these forest areas, good work has been done by our Forest Service to keep up our heritage. Many acres have been made into parks, where it is hoped the trees will be safe and enjoyed for years to come.

Many acres of forest land have been bought by the government and set aside as National Forests, too. People fought this idea at first. They did not want the government to interfere with their cutting. They wanted all the forests to use as they wished. But under President Benjamin Harrison a bill was passed by which thirteen million acres became National Forest land.

Not much was done with this land until Teddy

Roosevelt became president. During his administration, the thirteen million acres became one hundred and twenty million acres of National Forest. And all this was protected by the government under the Department of Agriculture.

Another Roosevelt—Franklin D.—carried on the good work. Of all our presidents, he was the most interested in National Forests. During the depression of 1929-35, when the price of land was low, he saw to it that fifty million dollars was used to buy up more land for National Forests. And during these years more good work was done in soil and forestry conservation than ever before or since.

For ten years boys in the CCC (Civilian Conservation Corps) worked on many forest projects. They planted over five million acres of farm wood lots, as well as large areas in public forests. They fought forest fires. They repaired many thousands of miles of old fire trails and roadways and built many thousands of miles of new ones. These fire trails and roadways are cleared passageways made through heavy brush and timber lands. They open up areas, otherwise inaccessible, for forest patrols, fire fighters, and their equipment. Ranger stations and telephone lines were built through the forests. Every state was helped by their work and nearly every national park and forest and many public campgrounds.

For example, they worked over and improved nearly four million acres of forest land in the Black Hills area alone. And about two million acres of new forests were planted on barren land in the Great Lakes region.

Under the Works Progress Administration a great "shelter belt" was built across the prairie states. Two hundred seventeen million trees were planted on more than thirty thousand farms. They form a forest windbreak of eighteen thousand six hundred miles to protect this great treeless tract from winds and drought.

Today the Forest Service takes care of the one hundred eighty-one million, one hundred fifty-one thousand acres of woodlands which make up our one hundred fifteen National Forests. It also guards against fire in just as many other millions of acres that are owned by private landowners.

In fact, much of our forest land is privately owned. That is, it is not owned by the government, but by farmers or by big lumber or paper companies. Some are big holdings—four hundred thousand acres or more. Most of them, however, are small farm wood lots of forty acres or so. The Forest Service

MAKING OUR BARREN LANDS GREEN

men advise the owners how best to care for their forest lands and wood lots.

Today many trees are grown as crops. When forests are cared for properly, the trees can be grown and cut in such a way that they will grow continuously year after year, yet there will always be trees to cut.

The pioneers had no such ideas. They cut trees from the forest much as we get minerals from a mine. They cleaned out the forests and then moved on. "Cut out and get out" was the way they did it. Now we know we must cut carefully from our forests if we want them to last.

Men of the Forest Service have been doing a fine job in teaching the people how best to do this. Many of the big lumber and pulp companies teach proper forest methods, too. They know they must keep their trees growing if they are going to have trees to use.

Over twenty-five hundred tree farms have been set up in many of our states. These farms are sponsored in each state by some well-known forest agency. On each tree farm the owner promises his sponsor to cut his trees properly, so as to keep the trees always growing. He promises to protect the trees from fire, insects, and disease.

The lumbering is done scientifically. The work is done so as not to harm the rest of the forest. Trees are cut when they are "ripe," or ready for cutting. Young trees are left to mature. Only part of the older trees are taken. Others are left in spots where the wind can scatter their seeds and start whole new forest sections. A tree farm certificate is given each farm when an examining forester finds the owner is living up to the rules. The certificate is withdrawn if at any time the owner backslides.

The Forest Service also encouraged the replanting of idle, barren land which had once been cleared by the pioneers for farming. After clearing it, the farmers found that it was not good for their crops and left it barren and idle. It was, however, suited to growing trees. So the great task of replanting these acres in forest is going forward.

Other tree planting is being done by the American Forestry Association. "One billion trees on one million acres a year!" That is their slogan. They have been planting millions of trees in state forests. Private landowners and big companies are doing their part, too. They have planted across many vacant areas and scattered seeds by helicopter and by hand over miles of idle land. Even so, the forests are still being used up faster than they are being regrown.

There are four and one-fourth million little forests in our country. Many of the owners are using their wood lots properly. But on more than two-thirds of these wood lots the trees are still being improperly cut with little or no thought of regrowing, replanting, or replacing "firewood" trees with "timber" trees.

The great question is, can these farmers be educated to do as they should of their own free will? Or must they be made to do so by force? In some of the states, force is now being used. But this still is not enough. Perhaps federal laws will have to be passed to protect every forest in the land, no matter who owns it. This may be necessary in spite of all the good work being done.

6

SOFTWOOD TREES THAT GIVE US LUMBER

Just about every part of a tree is now put to use by mankind—leaves, sap, bark, limbs, trunk, even the roots. It would take pages to list all the things now made from trees. And there are new things being added every year.

Everything from smoking pipes to sealing wax, crayons, tanks, hats, rugs, combs, napkin rings, phonograph records, dolls, buttons, lampshades—on and on. Surely there has not been one hour since you were born when you have not used, or come in contact with, some product of the tree.

Perhaps the most important material we get from trees is wood. And the foremost use of wood is in lumber and building. The trees most needed for this

SOFTWOOD TREES THAT GIVE US LUMBER

are the softwoods. Their big, tall trunks can be sawed into very strong beams and boards. This saw timber or sawed lumber, as it is called, is used in much of the heavy building we do.

Softwoods give us more than three-fourths of all our sawed lumber. Our biggest and most important timber trees are now in the forests of the West. One of the best timber trees is the Douglas fir. Authorities tell us there is more standing saw timber in Douglas fir than in any other species.

The Douglas fir is a curious tree. It is unlike any other softwood known. It's a mixed-up sort of tree—not really a true fir at all. Its trunk has deep furrows like that of a fir tree, but its cones hang down like those of a spruce. And its needles are fastened to the twig by a tiny stem, as are those of a hemlock.

Scientists find this tree quite puzzling. They do not know exactly what to call it. Some call it Douglas fir, some call it Douglas spruce. Others have named it the Douglas tree. Even the botanical name of this big, handsome tree shows how puzzled everyone is. It is called *Pseudotsuga taxifolia*, which means "false hemlock with a yewlike leaf." The needles do look like those of a yew.

The Douglas fir cones are different, too, from any other cones in the world. Growing out from each

cone scale is a little three-pointed leaf or *bract*. These bracts stretching out from the scales are soft and green. They give the brown cones a colorful, feathery look.

Except for the sequoia, the Douglas fir is our largest forest tree. It is one hundred and eighty to two hundred and fifty feet tall, and from four to eight feet thick. It grows thickly in great forests in the Pacific Northwest and can be found in some parts of every one of our western states, as well as in Canada and Mexico.

SOFTWOOD TREES THAT GIVE US LUMBER

The trees grow fast and are quite hardy. They are long-lived, too—from one hundred to three hundred years or more. The rings on some of the trees that have been cut show they had been growing for five hundred years!

People plant this tree—in Europe as well as in America—to decorate their grounds and cities. When grown this way it does not have to vie with other trees in a forest for room and nourishment, so it looks even prettier. Soft branches start low on the trunk, fairly sweeping the ground. They lift up in green and graceful beauty. When young they have a gay Christmas-tree look. And out west they are quite often used as Christmas trees, too.

The western yellow pine is another fine timber tree. It's also called the ponderosa pine *(Pinus ponderosa)*. You find it growing in every western state, as well as in parts of Mexico and Canada. In fact, it is able to grow over a wider range than any other softwood in our country—from sea level to mountain slopes twelve thousand feet high.

The ponderosa pine gets to be quite old—from two hundred fifty to five hundred years. And, strangely enough, the older it grows the more handsome it becomes.

Up to one hundred years, the "young" trees are

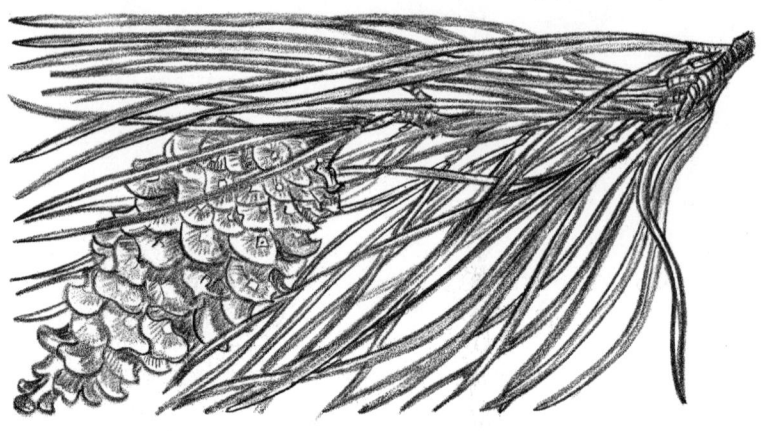

not especially outstanding. But once they get to be a hundred some amazing changes take place. The dull brown or black color of the bark fades away. Gay shades of yellow, orange, russet brown or cinnamon red appear. The furrows in the trunk fill out and divide into big, smooth sections or plates.

Now the tree looks handsome, indeed. Surely it is king of the forest—in beauty of bark, at least. No other western pine can compare with its splendor. And gay and handsome it remains, all the rest of its life.

Eight southern relatives of the ponderosa are fine timber trees, also. These are the southern yellow pines. They lead all other softwoods in the amount of lumber they give us. At least one-third of all the lumber cut in the United States is southern pine.

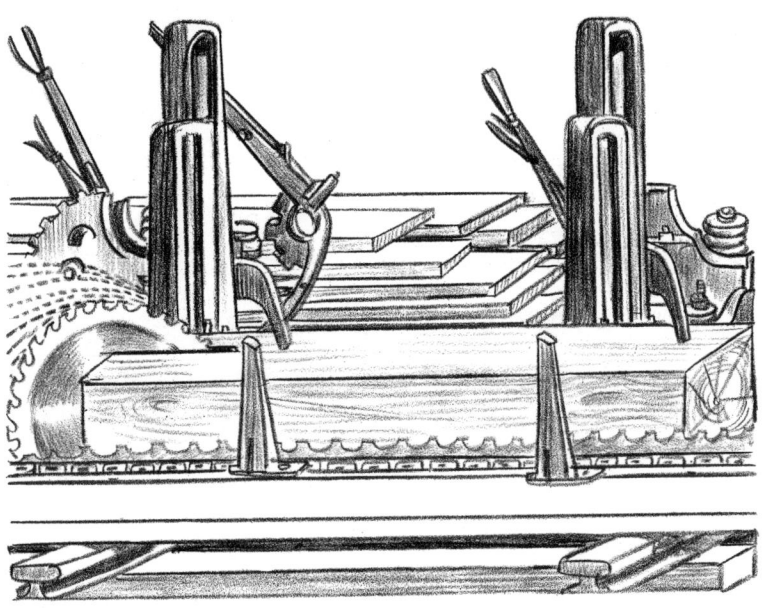

Four of the eight are especially outstanding in this respect. They are the longleaf, shortleaf, loblolly, and slash pines.

The longleaf pine *(Pinus palustris)* certainly lives up to its name. Its needles are longer than those of any other pine in the world—up to eighteen inches. They are a shining dark green and are grouped three to a bundle, held at the base by a beautiful silvery sheath.

The cones are long, too—up to ten inches. The bark, as in other yellow pines, is red or orange. It's such a pretty tree the young saplings often have been cut and used for Christmas trees.

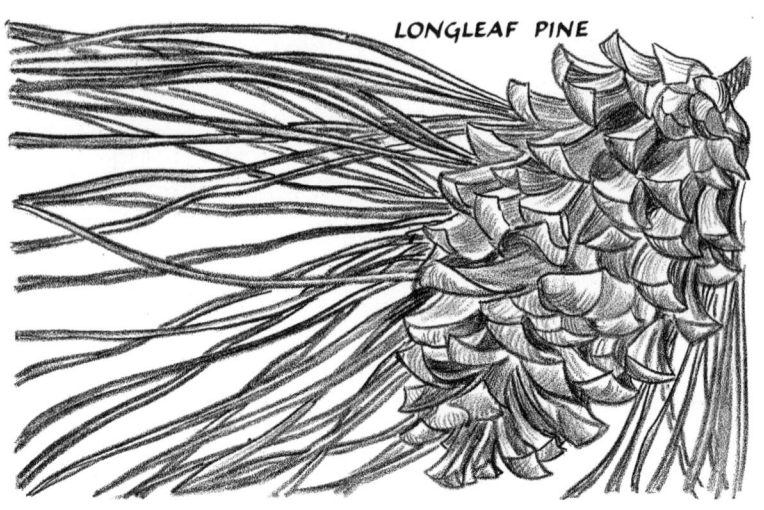
LONGLEAF PINE

The longleaf is also an important source of resin and turpentine. It's a tall tree, reaching to one hundred twenty feet, and is found from southern Virginia to Florida and west to Texas.

The shortleaf pine *(Pinus echinata)* is also like its name. The needles are short—three to five inches long. They are dark bluish-green and grow in bundles of two or three. The brown cones are shorter, too—about two inches long. And the tree does not grow as tall as the longleaf—around sixty to ninety feet.

The shortleaf grows from Pennsylvania to northern Florida and west to Texas.

The slash pine *(Pinus caribaea)* is one of the most important trees of the South. It is one of the pret-

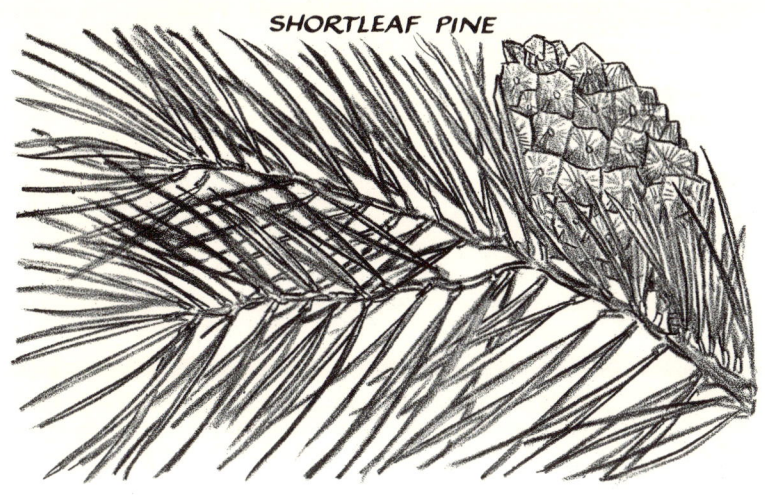

SHORTLEAF PINE

tiest, too, and many people plant it around their homes and streets.

The slash pine grows from the southern section of South Carolina through Florida and west to Louisiana. It grows best (up to one hundred fifty feet) in swampy land. People of the South call their swamps "slashes." That is why this tree is called the slash pine.

The loblolly pine *(Pinus taeda)* gets its name from its habit of growing in low, moist places. The southern people call these low spots "loblollies." So they named this pine the loblolly.

There's another interesting thing about this tree. It can take over bare, abandoned fields and make them green again. It is very good at this, too, because it is a fast-growing tree. Most pines drop their seeds only every second year. But the loblolly drops its seeds every year.

The seeds take root and grow very easily. Once some of the seeds get started, it isn't too long before these remarkable trees turn the bare field into a thriving young forest.

The loblolly grows near the coast from New Jersey to Florida and along the Gulf Coast to eastern Texas.

In the early days of our country the lumber from virgin forests of loblolly was among the finest in the world. It was in great demand by shipbuilders when the great white pine began to give out. But these huge, century-old pines have long since gone. The trees growing now are second growth trees and smaller—sixty to one hundred feet tall. But for lumber and paper making, the loblolly is still one of the South's important products.

7

HARDWOOD TREES THAT GIVE US LUMBER

CONIFERS give us three-fourths of our sawed lumber, and the other one-fourth comes from hardwoods. A great many different kinds of hardwood trees make up this one-fourth.

Wood of the ash tree, for instance, is very hard and tough. It makes strong handles for shovels, rakes, forks, and hoes. Furniture-makers like walnut, birch, sweet gum, maple, and oak. Paper companies use a great deal of poplar. But the most important timber trees in the hardwood family are probably the white and red oaks and the sugar maple.

Wood of the sugar maple *(Acer saccharum)* is very hard. The word *Acer* means hard or sharp. In ancient times weapons were made from maple. Now

the wood is used in making high-grade furniture, flooring, toys, musical instruments, and many other expensive articles.

The second part of the botanical name, *saccharum*, means sweet. This is because of the sweet sap and the delicious maple syrup we get from the sugar maple. Strangely enough, though the sap from the maple tree is sweet, it does not have any maple flavor. The true, delicious maple flavor must be developed by boiling the sap.

Indians were the first to tap our sugar maples. They made a gash in the tree, stuck in a funnel made from bark, and caught the sap in buckets made from bark. Then they dropped hot stones into the liquid to boil the sap down to syrup.

There's an interesting legend about how the

HARDWOOD TREES THAT GIVE US LUMBER

Indians first learned to make maple syrup. A squaw boiled her moose meat in a kettle filled with sap from a nearby sugar maple. While her meat was boiling she visited with a neighbor. She was horrified when she returned to find the liquid had boiled down to a sticky mess around the moose meat.

She hid when she heard her husband returning for dinner, afraid of his anger. Peering out from her hiding place, she watched him taste the sticky mess. To her surprise, she saw him lick his fingers in delight, then dig in for more and more, quite forgetting the burned meat.

When she dared come out he praised her for the wonderful new treat she had cooked for him. And, from that time, so the story goes, we have enjoyed maple syrup and maple sugar.

The Indians taught the white man how to tap the maple trees in early spring, when the days were warm but the nights still cold. Surely every boy and girl who has lived in sugar maple country knows about "sugaring-off" time.

The maple syrup is carefully boiled to just the right consistency, then poured in bite-size portions onto pans of clean, white snow. On the cold snow it quickly congeals into a caramel-like wax, ready to be poked up and popped into waiting mouths. No one who ever has tasted it can forget its warm-cold richness, its sweet melting delight on the tongue.

The sugar maple is a handsome tree from seventy to one hundred and twenty-five feet in height, with a trunk two or three feet thick. Its buds, leaves, and branches grow opposite one another in a neat pattern.

It's a pretty tree during every season of the year. In the spring, greenish-yellow flowers dangle daintily in clusters. And tiny new leaves spread over the tree. Soon the flowers fade, and the leaves grow big —four to five inches across.

HARDWOOD TREES THAT GIVE US LUMBER

The fruits are winged seeds. Maple "keys" they are called, because they look like little keys hanging down. They ripen in the fall and sail easily away on the wind. In the fall, too, the leaves turn all the countryside into a glorious blaze of color. Deep red, yellow, orange, and scarlet flame against the autumn sky. The colors of the maple seem brighter and clearer than those of any other tree in America.

There are about thirteen different species of maple trees native to the United States. Each is a fine tree in its own special way. But the sugar maple is the most useful, most beautiful, and most plentiful of all. Surely it's the queen of our forests. And it is found in every state from the Great Plains east to the Atlantic.

If the sugar maple seems to be queen, we can call the oak tree king. For one thing there are more kinds of oaks in the world than any other tree, and they furnish some of the finest timber. For another, it is a magnificent tree—huge, wide-spreading, handsome, and strong. "Strong as an oak" is an old saying. Or "brave men with hearts of oak." Even its botanical name shows what people think of it—*Quercus* means "fine tree."

Of all the oaks, the two most valuable lumber trees are the white oak and the red oak.

The white oak *(Quercus alba)* grows naturally in the eastern half of the United States—from southern Canada, Minnesota, and Nebraska south to Florida and Texas. People love it for its beauty and its hard wood. Many of our wooden ships in the early days

WHITE OAK

were built of white oak—just one of a thousand things it has been used for down the years.

This oak grows straight and tall—seventy to one hundred feet—with a trunk two to three feet thick. Its strong limbs stretch out, often fifty feet or more, providing great areas of cooling shade. Below ground its sturdy roots spread almost as wide. You seldom see these great oaks blown down.

Like most eastern hardwoods, this oak is deciduous. It loses its leaves in the autumn. In the spring the new leaves are a bright, shiny red at first, turning to pink, then silvery white. And underneath they're covered with soft, velvety hairs.

The early settlers watched these oaks and planted their corn when the pink-silvery leaves were the size of a squirrel's ears. They built their homes where the white oaks grew. They knew the soil there would be good and rich.

In the fall the oak leaves turn deep red and purple. The acorns ripen and make feasts for the birds and squirrels.

When you find acorns on a white oak you know it is at least fifty years old. It takes that long for the tree to bear fruit. But this is still young for the white oak, which lives to be two thousand years old.

A western cousin, the Oregon white oak *(Quercus garryana)* is the best timber oak of the Northwest, with wood that is hard and strong. It is a smaller tree—fifty to ninety feet tall—and its light, gray-brown bark is sometimes nearly white.

It grows in a limited area—from Vancouver

Island, British Columbia, south into western Washington and Oregon to the Santa Cruz Mountains in central California.

The red oak *(Quercus borealis)* is native to the eastern half of the United States and nearby Canada. This oak was little appreciated in the early days. The eastern white oak was the popular tree then. Not until the white oak began to be scarce did its red oak cousin come into its own.

The wood of the red oak is hard and strong. And, best of all, the tree is very fast growing. Most of the valuable oaks, in contrast, are slow growing. The red oak is sixty to one hundred feet tall, rugged and sturdy, with short, stout branches that are straighter than those of the white oak.

Oak leaves are interesting because they differ from one another, even on the same tree. This is especially true of the red oak leaves. They vary so much it is hard to describe them exactly. However, there are two things you can always look for in identifying these leaves. Both the lobes and the spaces between the lobes are mostly triangular. And each lobe ends in a sharp point or bristle. In the spring the new leaves are lined with a soft whitish down. In the fall the leaves turn a deep red.

The large, plump acorns are pretty but very bitter. Even the squirrels leave them strictly alone.

The oak has been loved and admired all down the ages. In the olden days people used to think the oak was the home of their gods. Important problems were solved by drawing lots from an urn placed under an oak. Or by listening to the rustling of the leaves. They thought the gods talked to them that way.

Sometimes the people would cut a cross in the tree's bark. They thought this gave them protection from their enemies. And they would eat the acorns to get wisdom.

In some countries people believed fairies lived in the trunks of the oaks. They thought these fairies went in and out through holes left where branches had fallen. Sick people would touch these "fairy doors" to be healed. Or they would fasten locks of their hair to the tree, or carry bits of its bark.

Even here in our own country, in colonial days, the sick were sometimes pushed through a fork in the tree by superstitious folk who believed this would cure them.

The Indians showed our pioneers how to use the acorns for food. They soaked the bitterness out of the acorns and pounded them into a coarse meal.

The oak is often mentioned in the Bible. Many

important happenings took place under an oak. Many deaths, burials, visions, and the performance of idolatrous rites occurred "under an oak." The bodies of Saul and his sons were buried "under the oak in Jabesh" (I Chron. 10:12). And it was "under an oak which was in Ophrah" that an angel appeared to Gideon commanding him to save Israel from the Midianites (Judges 6:11).

Oaks have played a part in the history of our country. There was the Charter Oak at Hartford. The charter of the Colony of Connecticut was hidden in a hollow of the trunk of this tree when James II tried to take their charter from the settlers.

And there is the great oak in Friend's Cemetery at Salem, New Jersey, under whose huge branches Washington's soldiers drilled. The Wadsworth Oak near Genessee, New York, was called "The Big Tree" by the Indians and early settlers. And under it, in 1797, an important treaty was made by Robert Morris and the Seneca Indians.

Almost every state and many of our towns and cities have a special oak of which they are particularly proud. And they have many oaks which they love and admire.

It is no wonder. The oak is a magnificent tree. We must protect it whenever we can.

8

TREES THAT GIVE US FUEL

Although the greatest use of wood is lumber for building, wood for fuel runs a very close second. Over one-fourth of all the wood we use each year is for fuel.

More than sixty million cords of wood are burned in the United states each year for fuel. Probably about one-third of this wood is waste from industries which manufacture things from wood. They are able to use their own wood waste for the fuel they need. Wood waste consists of such leftover pieces as slabs, trimmings, and edgings. Even sawdust and shavings are used. When formed into briquets they make a fine, clean fuel.

Wood for fuel comes from all kinds of trees, generally those that are most plentiful in each part of

TREES THAT GIVE US FUEL

the country. These are usually trees that are not especially valuable in any other way—such as the scrub oaks and pitch pines along our Atlantic Coast.

The most plentiful trees, however, do not necessarily make the best fuel. A good fuel wood is heavy, so it burns longer and gives off more heat. Some of the favorite fuel trees are the black locust, hickory, elm, maple, birch, beech, cherry, and ash. In California the eucalyptus and oak are also good for fuel.

Among the fuel trees, black locust is tops. This interesting tree grew at first only in a small section of our southern Appalachian valleys. Early settlers enjoyed its pretty leaves and fragrant, white, wistarialike blossoms. They planted it wherever they went. So now the black locust *(Robinia pseudoacacia)* is found in every state east of the Mississippi, except Florida, and in some of the western states.

It is a tree of medium size—up to eighty feet tall —with a trunk twelve to thirty-six inches thick. The new leaves are a bright yellow-green and have a very unusual habit. Every night, and whenever it rains, they fold up as though going to sleep.

Wood of the black locust is very tough and long lasting. The colonists made wooden pegs from this wood to use in building their homes and ships. Today, because this wood can stand up under all kinds of wear and weather, pins are made from it to hold the glass insulators of telephone wires.

Black locust wood makes the finest fuel of any wood we have. It is hard to start, but when it does get going it burns like coal, with a bright blue flame. A cord, when properly dried, is almost equal to one ton of hard coal.

It could be a useful timber tree, too. Unfortunately, however, the locust beetle bores through the bark and into the heartwood, spoiling the tree for lumber. Many of the trees are killed by these insects and by fungus attack. Nevertheless, the black locust is helpful in reclaiming and reforesting land.

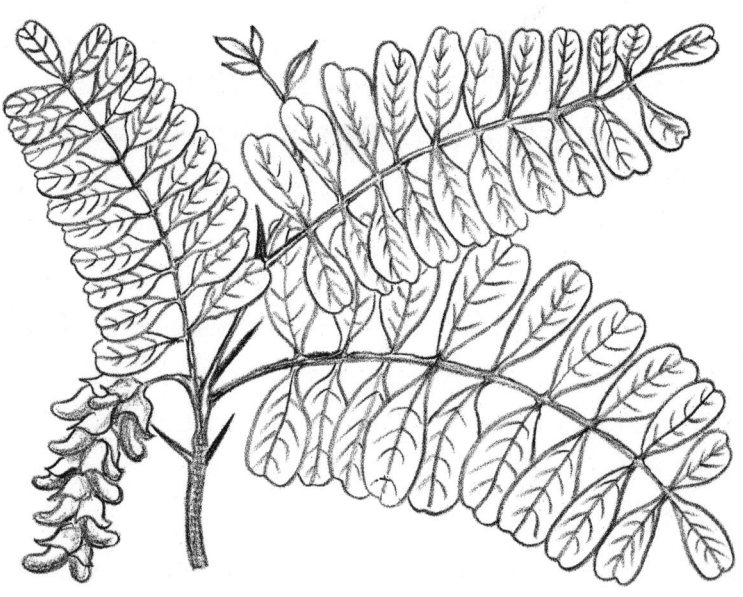

A close second to the black locust in fuel value is the hickory, particularly the shagbark hickory *(Carya ovata)*. This strong, sturdy tree, with its interesting shaggy bark, grows to one hundred twenty feet.

Ever since pioneer days it has been a great favorite. Many of the log cabins of the early settlers were kept warm, night and day, by great logs of shagbark hickory burning in their fireplaces. They used its wood to fence in their lands and to make ramrods for their guns, hoops for their barrels, and hinges for their cabin doors.

The name "Old Hickory" was given to General

Andrew Jackson in admiration for his tough strength. "Tough as hickory," they put it. Today Jackson's grave at "The Hermitage" in Tennessee is shaded by six great shagbark hickory trees.

The colonists prized the nuts from this tree, too. The Indians taught them to pound the nuts into a meal, which they tossed into boiling water. As the oily paste came to the surface it was carefully strained off, and it was sweet and rich as cream. They called it hickory milk, and they used it in their cooking.

Lighter woods are used for fuel, too—trees such as cedar, spruce, soft pine, redwood, cypress, aspen, basswood, and poplar. But these have only about half as much heat value as those in the heavier wood group. A cord of this softer wood will give about as much heat as one-half ton of coal.

In the South people burn softwoods that are rich in resin. The resin in the wood flames up so quickly and easily there is no need to use paper or kindling to set it afire.

Wood for fuel has been important through the years, and it continues to be so. Several million Americans still use wood to heat their homes and to cook their meals, in spite of our modern gas, oil, and electricity. And we all love to toast our toes

TREES THAT GIVE US FUEL

beside crackling logs burning in a blazing fireplace.

In fact, wood will probably become even more important as chemists constantly find new uses for it. They have turned wood into such things as alcohol for liquid fuel and gas for motor fuel.

Firewood is important in other countries, too. Two-thirds of the human race still use wood for fuel. Fifty-seven per cent of the wood produced by all the forests of the world is burned for fuel.

Some countries have thoughtlessly destroyed nearly all their forests in search of fuel they needed so badly. China is such a country. Greece is another. Greece was once heavily forested along its mountain slopes and lovely valleys, but two-thirds of its forest land was ruined by ruthless cutting and the later erosion by floods. Crete, once famous for its forests of cypress and cedar, became a stony waste which couldn't even hold the winter rains.

In fact, two-thirds of Europe was once fine forest land. Less than one half of these original forests remain. Floods and famine have been the results in many countries because of deforestation.

The lesson for us in these tragedies is obvious.

9

TREES THAT GIVE US PAPER

ONE authority, who likes to figure, says there are more than nine thousand ways in which we use paper! Chances are we couldn't name these nine thousand uses. But we do know paper plays a big part in our daily lives.

Back in history, people carved on stone and wrote on the leaves and bark of trees. Then they made a kind of paper, called papyrus, from the spongy part of a plant. Later they learned to make paper from cotton and linen rags. But this was expensive, and the rags were not always easy to get.

Not so many years ago paper was very scarce, even in this country, because it had to be made from rags. This paper was very high grade. If you will look at a book published in the seventeenth century, you can see that its pages are as fine as writing paper.

TREES THAT GIVE US PAPER

Because this fine paper was so scarce and expensive, our ancestors wrote on slates when they went to school. They would have been shocked at the way we waste paper today. And think how amazed they would have been at the thought of using paper napkins, paper towels, or paper handkerchiefs!

Then, in the nineteenth century, we learned an important lesson from the wasps and hornets. A French scientist named Reaumur, watching these insects at work, noticed how they chewed woody fiber and let it dry into a papery sort of material with which they made their nests. Paper from wood! An idea was born. If wasps and hornets could do it, why couldn't man?

And before long we were doing just that. A paper machine was invented, and paper was being made from wood pulp in France and England.

We first began doing this in our country in 1869. Only a little was made at first. But it was successful. Gradually we made more and more paper from wood pulp. We found better and better ways of making it. But even today much of the paper is made in the same general way used by the wasps and hornets.

Scientists discovered how to take the wood apart with chemicals. In this way they were able to sep-

OUR AMERICAN TREES

arate the cellulose—one of the things the tree makes from sunshine, air, and water—from the rest of the substances in wood.

This was a great event. Chemists then found they could work with the cellulose in many ways. They discovered how to make many products from it—from soda straws to gunpowder, salad bowls, shoe soles, and carpets. But of them all, paper is the most important.

At least thirty-one different kinds of trees are now being used to make paper. Scientists tell us many other kinds of trees can be used, if we need them, by making a few simple changes in the manufacturing processes.

Wood is turned into paper in four different ways. The variety of wood makes this necessary. Southern pines, for instance, could not be used to make paper at first because there was so much resin in the wood. Chemists found a way to overcome this. Now these trees, too, are an important source of paper.

About ninety per cent of the wood used in making paper comes from softwoods. These include spruce, balsam, fir, western hemlock, and pine. The other ten per cent comes from the wood of about eighteen different hardwood trees. The most important in this group are the various kinds of poplars.

Next come the beech, birch, maple, sweet gum, and tupelo. Then the ash, elm, willow, oak, and chestnut.

However, one tree stands out above all the rest when it comes to making paper. Its soft woody fibers have just the right texture, and it has very little resin. It is the white spruce *(Picea glauca)*, a tree that can rightly be called the pulpwood king.

White spruce is a handsome tree of the northern forests. It grows from Newfoundland and Labrador to Alaska, south to British Columbia, Montana, Minnesota, Wisconsin, Michigan, and on through all our northeastern states.

The trees grow forty to ninety feet tall and have a graceful, tapering form. The trunk is one to two feet thick. The needles crowd closely around the twigs and are almost curly. The tree is thickly covered with branches which sweep down and then turn up gracefully at the ends.

The needles are four-sided, stiff, and less than an inch long. They are blue-green, often with a pale bluish-white tint. It is this which gives the white spruce its name.

There is one sure way you can tell a white spruce from all the other spruces. Just crush a twig or needle in your hand and smell it. If you feel like holding your nose and saying, "Phew!"—it's a white spruce.

Some people call it the "cat tree" because of this polecat smell.

A close relative, the Black Hills spruce *(Picea glauca albertiana)* is found in South Dakota, Wyoming, Montana, and Alberta, Canada. You might call it "Big Brother Albert," because it's a taller, bigger

TREES THAT GIVE US PAPER

tree than the rest of the white spruces. It towers to one hundred fifty feet, often tapering to a narrow, more pointed top. Its trunk is four to five feet thick.

Immense forests of white spruce rise green and beautiful across parts of Canada. And it is from these forests a great deal of our paper comes. Our own trees cannot begin to furnish us with all the pulpwood we need. In fact, many of the large newspapers in our country own spruce forests in Canada. By replanting and proper forestry methods these trees are kept growing to furnish much of the paper we need.

It takes eighty acres of woodland *every week* to furnish enough paper to keep one of our big New York daily papers going! Yet paper for printing is just a small part of the paper we use every day— only about one fourth.

We use, in fact, over twenty million tons of paper a year. Think of the trees it must take to furnish wood pulp for the thousands of other ways in which we use paper: all the boxes and cartons our groceries come packaged in; the paper napkins, towels, handkerchiefs, cups, plates, forks, and spoons; the writing paper we use and the wrapping paper and fiberboard —on and on.

No wonder we need to guard our forests.

10

TREES THAT GIVE US CLOTH

It was the wasps and hornets that first gave us the idea for making paper from wood. And it was the silkworm that taught us how to make rayon!

A Frenchman, Count Hilaire de Chardonnet, studied the silkworm at work. He saw how the worm ate mulberry leaves, digested them, and turned them into a sticky jelly. This sticky jelly was forced out through tiny holes in the silkworm's body. When it hit the air it hardened into thin, shiny threads. He thought about this process and decided that perhaps the same process might be gone through in a laboratory.

As a result of his observations, we make rayon from wood in much the same way as the silkworm

TREES THAT GIVE US CLOTH

does. But we use cellulose instead of mulberry leaves. Cellulose is made into a jelly; and this jelly, when forced through tiny holes, comes out a shining thread—a thread which can be woven into a cloth as lovely as silk. This is how rayon is made. And our chemists have become expert in spinning it into very fine threads—so fine, in fact, they tell us it takes a thousand miles of it to weigh one pound.

Now as long as we care for our forests and keep our trees growing, we can have all the silky rayon we need—from wood. And we need a great deal. The rayon yarn and fiber industry has become tremendously important. By 1949 we were turning out more than seven hundred and fifty million dollars worth of rayon products each year. And the industry is constantly growing. About ninety per cent of the fibrous material used in these rayon products is wood pulp.

Motion picture film is made from cellulose jelly, too. And all kinds of plastic things.

It is the western hemlock in particular that gives us the kind of wood we need to make cellulose jelly. In fact, the western hemlock *(Tsuga heterophylla)* might be called a Cinderella tree. For many years its wood was thought of little use. Then someone discovered that it made fine flooring, furniture, and paneling. Next they found it made fine paper pulp.

Then one day it made really big news! Western hemlock was found to have qualities no other wood seemed to have, and these qualities were just what was needed for making rayon, cellophane, and plastics.

Now many of the things you wear and use every day of your life are products of this western hemlock. When you pull on a rayon dress or shirt you are pulling on a bit of western hemlock. The plastic toys you play with, the buttons on your clothes, the cellophane wrapper around your new sweater—all are made from hemlock. True, it isn't the only tree that gives us these things, but it is the most important.

The western hemlock is a tall tree, reaching to one hundred eighty feet in the northwestern forests. And its trunk is about four feet thick. It needs moisture and rain and a rather mild climate, so the northwest coastal forests suit it well. It grows beautifully in the small fog-belt section along the coast of northern California, where it is often called the coast hemlock. It thrives in higher elevations, too—up to six thousand feet in the northern Rocky Mountain region south to Idaho and Montana.

Its glossy, yellowish-green needles are narrow and flat and grooved on the upper surface. They are

about one-quarter to seven-eighths inch long. The reddish-brown cones are small—three-quarters inch to one-and-a-quarter inches long—and they hang down from the branches.

Decorative and useful—that is the western hemlock!

11

TREES THAT GIVE US CHEMICALS

REMEMBER, when you step out proudly in your new leather shoes that the trees had a part in making them! Tannin is an important substance in the shrinking and seasoning of leather. And tannin is extracted from wood.

It is found in the bark of many trees, and helps protect the trees against the ravages of destructive insects.

The art of getting tannin from trees to use in preserving leather has been known for centuries. Records show that the Chinese used this method over three thousand years ago. And well-turned-out leather articles, dating back about as far, have been found in Egyptian tombs. Early Virginia settlers

TREES THAT GIVE US CHEMICALS

built the first tannery in America in 1630, soon after they arrived.

Three of the most important trees from which we get tannin are the oak, hemlock, and chestnut. It is tannin that makes the oak tree's acorns so bitter. And tannin makes up about half of the "oak apples" you sometimes see as a growth on oak trees.

Tannin makes up as much as thirteen per cent of the bark of the hemlock. The chestnut, besides having tannin in its bark, has it in the wood, too. This has made the chestnut especially valuable in the leather industry.

It was a great loss when most of these grand old trees were killed by a chestnut blight that swept the country. Nothing was found to save these trees, and the new sprouts refused to grow back. But even the dead trees served mankind, for chemists were able to extract tannin from their bark and wood.

The longleaf and slash pines of the South give us turpentine and rosin. These valuable chemicals are called *naval stores*. Long ago we used pitch and tar from these trees to calk the seams of our wooden sailing vessels. Now that ships are made of steel, we no longer need naval stores for this purpose. However, the old name still remains.

We use naval stores in many products—paints,

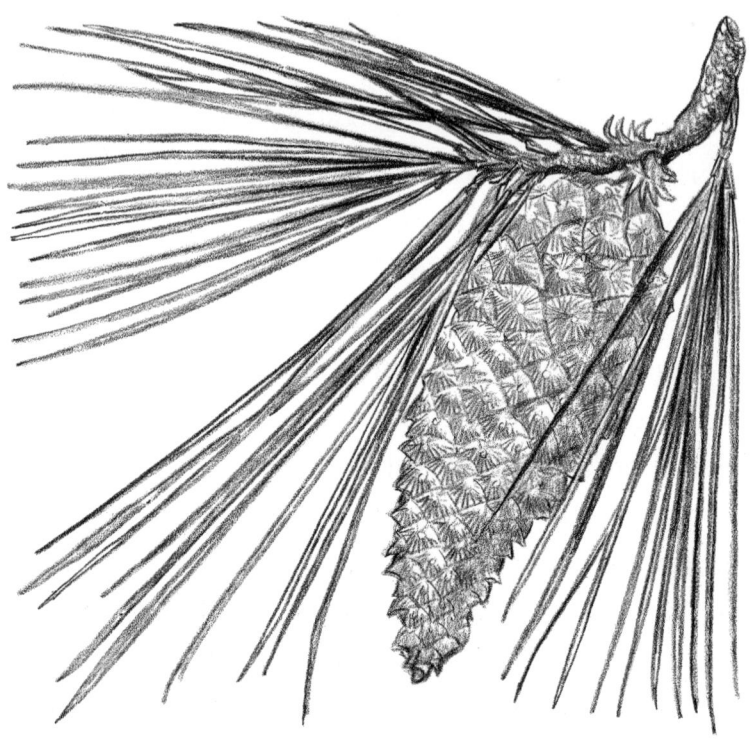

soaps, varnishes, sealing waxes, plastics, synthetic rubber, flypaper—things that we use every day of our lives.

Turpentine and rosin are taken from stumps of southern pines that have been cut for lumber. They are also taken from the living trees.

Men make small cuts in the bark of the trees and fasten clay or galvanized iron cups below the cut. The cups hold about one quart and take from two to five weeks to fill. The liquid substance is a soft gum

TREES THAT GIVE US CHEMICALS

called oleoresin, which is processed into turpentine and rosin.

Trees such as the southern pines are able to give us this gum because they have an extra network of pipelines that run up and down the trees and back and forth crosswise. The living cells of which these pipelines are built give off the gum.

The tree uses this gum to heal injuries, sending it flowing through the pipelines toward any wound in its bark. Tiny drops spread over the wound and harden into a sort of new skin.

When men first found use for this oleoresin, or for the turpentine and rosin it contains, they wounded the trees to get it. They made great gashes through the bark and collected the gum as it rushed out to heal the gashes. This process of wounding the trees in order to get the naval stores is called chipping.

At first they made so many and such large gashes the pines were killed. Now they have better methods. They have learned how to gather gum, year after year, without killing the trees or hurting the wood—which later can be used for lumber. They now make small cuts in the bark, only about one-half inch high and deep, and get just as good yield of the precious oleoresin. This harvesting of naval stores has become a very big industry in the South.

Another useful gum, called *storax*, is gathered from a common hardwood called the sweet gum tree *(Liquidambar styraciflua)*. Storax is gathered in much the same way as the naval stores. It is used in making drugs, perfumes, incense, flavoring extracts, and adhesives.

This beautiful tree is also called *Liquidambar* because of the fragrant gum it gives off, and red gum because its heartwood is a pretty reddish color.

Sweet gum grows naturally from Connecticut and New York west to Ohio, Illinois, Missouri, and Oklahoma, and south to Florida and Texas. It has been planted in other states, too—as far west as California—because of its beauty. Its star-shaped leaves turn bright shades of red, orange, and yellow in the fall.

Gum from four other trees is used in industry. Spruce gum goes into the manufacture of chewing gum, drugs, and confections. Resin from the Jeffrey pine and Digger pine gives a product called heptane, used to some extent as a measure for testing antiknock gasoline. Resin of the balsam fir is used in making drugs, adhesives, varnishes, and glass cement.

Ever since men found they could break wood apart with chemicals they have been carrying on

TREES THAT GIVE US CHEMICALS

interesting experiments. Year after year new ways have been found to turn wood of all kinds into sugar, ethyl alcohol, molasses, charcoal, tar, acetic acid, dyes, and oils. Every year brings forth the new products, developed by chemists from wood.

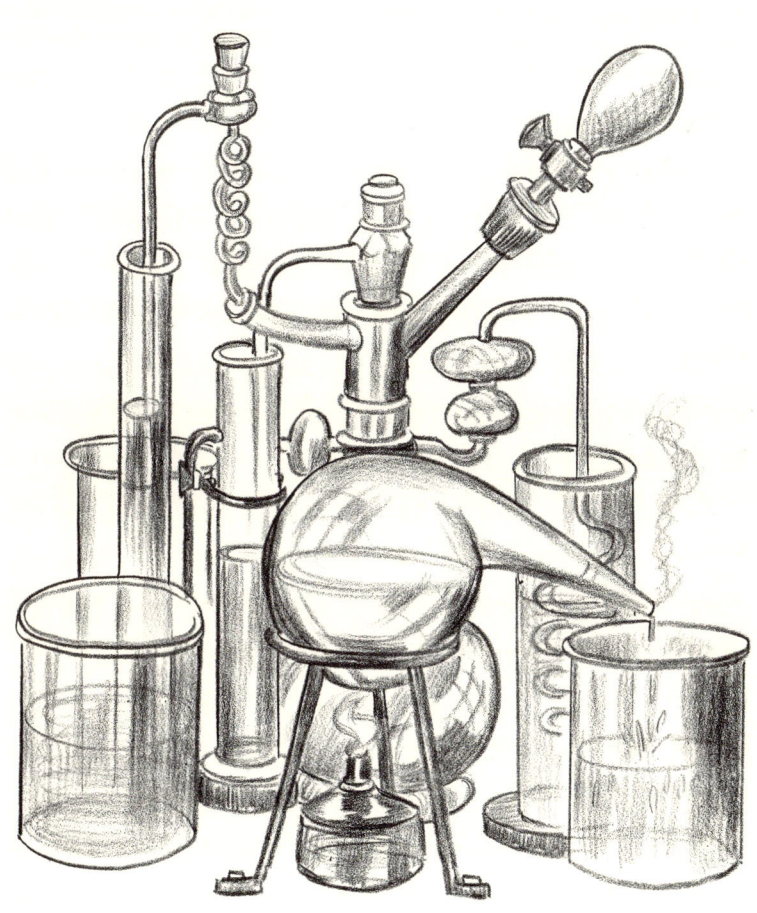

12

TREES THAT GIVE US FOOD

We can divide the trees that give us food into two classes—the orchard trees and the forest trees. Or, you might say, trees that are cultivated and trees that grow wild.

Perhaps there are fruit trees growing in your own back yard: apple, peach, plum—or, if you live in the South, orange trees. Or you may have nut trees: walnut, pecan, or hickory.

These are orchard fruit and nut trees. Someone has planted them, they have been carefully grown and cared for. These cultivated trees furnish an important part of our food.

Trees growing wild in the forests give us food, too. These are trees that no one has planted or cared for. There are millions of such trees throughout the country. They give us both nuts and fruit and are a very important part of our food industry.

From these forest trees we get pecans, walnuts, butternuts, hickory nuts, beechnuts, chestnuts, chinquapins, filberts, and piñon nuts. We get different kinds of fruit, too, from the forest trees, fruit such as persimmons, pawpaws, crab apples, plums, cherries, chokeberries, serviceberries, mulberries, and elderberries. The sugar maple we read about in chapter VII is still another forest tree that gives us food —maple sugar.

In early days Indians and pioneers used all these forest foods, and more. They couldn't, of course,

CHESTNUT

PINYON

go to the corner market for their needs, as we do. Nor did the colonists have time at first to plant fruit and nut trees on their lands. They had to make use of everything in the woods that was edible. Even the inner bark was ground up and made into bread.

The leaves, stems, and buds of some trees—the sassafras and swamp bay, for instance—have been used to flavor food. Buds of basswood, redbud, yucca, and palm have been eaten. Different kinds of drinks have been made from the coffee tree, sumac, birch, sassafras, holly, basswood, hemlock, spruce, and Douglas fir.

One of the most famous of all our forest food

TREES THAT GIVE US FOOD

trees is the pecan tree. We are the only country in the world where the pecan tree grows naturally. *Carya illinoensis* is its botanical name, and it belongs to the hickory family. Its nuts, so scientists tell us, have the highest food value of any nut in the world.

The pecan is a big tree, growing ninety to one hundred and twenty feet tall. Its huge limbs spread wide, sometimes as much as one hundred feet across. And its trunk is often thirty feet around. It is found growing wild in the Mississippi Valley region—from Indiana to Wisconsin, Iowa, and Kansas, and southward to Alabama, Texas, and Mexico.

These huge nut-bearing trees were not put to use as soon as our eastern trees were because, of course, this part of the country was not settled as early. Later, when adventuresome fur trappers crossed the Alleghenies, they brought back some of these nuts with their furs. They called them "Mississippi nuts" or "Illinois nuts." People liked them so well they began to plant them in their orchards. This was the beginning of the cultivated or orchard pecan trees.

Later, when the pioneers settled in these interior regions, they were delighted to find wide areas of these huge pecan trees growing wild. They began harvesting the nuts at once, but in a most destructive

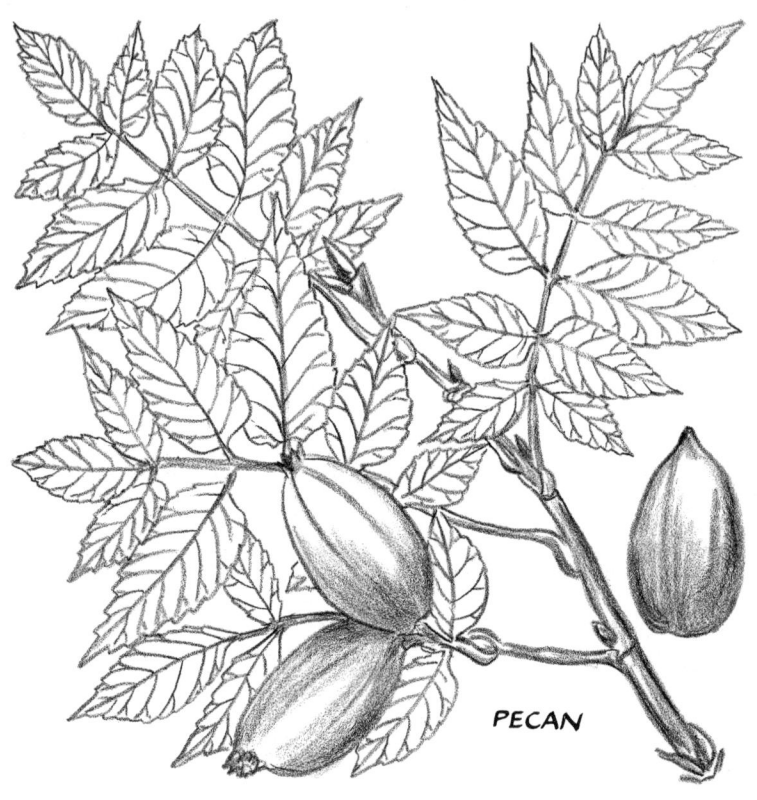

PECAN

way. Because it was hard to reach all the nuts on these big trees, they just cut the trees down right and left. It was like killing the goose that laid the golden egg!

They gave no thought to the years it had taken these trees to grow and bear fruit. Nor did they think about the future. Many of these fine old native pecans were destroyed before people realized what a senseless thing they were doing.

TREES THAT GIVE US FOOD

When they realized the value of the pecan trees they too started planting them in great orchards. Fortunately the pecan trees did well, not only in their own native sections but also in other states. They can grow where other fruit trees can not: in sections too far north for citrus fruit, for instance, and in sections too far south or in too low altitudes for apples and other deciduous fruit.

Now valuable orchards are thriving in many of our eastern and southern states, and even as far west as California and Oregon. There are two pecan trees still standing at Mount Vernon that have quite a history. They are said to have been started in 1785 by George Washington from nuts given him by Thomas Jefferson. They are thought to be the oldest trees at Mount Vernon.

One of the most important fruit trees is the apple. More than two hundred million bushels of apples are grown in North America each year. All these are from orchard-grown trees, because only apples from cultivated trees are good to eat.

We have many wild crab apple trees growing across our land. They are native to our country. They are lovely to look at, especially when in blossom; but the apples they bear are too sour to eat, except in jelly or cider. The Pilgrims found this out, much to their dismay, when they landed on our shores.

Later settlers brought their own "good eating" apple trees with them from Europe and planted them here in America. These trees thrived and before long we, too, boasted about our delicious eating apples.

You've probably read about Johnny Appleseed—how he roamed the countryside for forty years planting apple seeds, so everyone could enjoy these fine trees. Certainly he did a good job of getting his trees to grow. But he did not know that trees bearing good eating apples cannot be grown from seed. They revert back to the wild apple state too easily. So the trees that grew from the seeds he sowed bore sour apples.

However, they were strong, healthy trees, and the settlers soon learned how to use these wild trees to grow good apples. They did this by grafting on branches from orchard trees that were bearing sweet apples.

Since then the raising of apples has become a definite science. Now when a fine new apple is developed, sometimes after thirty or forty years of work, it is considered a very important event—so important, the new apple is registered in the patent office in Washington, D. C., just like a new invention!

13

OUR BIGGEST TREES

EVERY year thousands of people travel many miles to see the greatest tree giants in the world. And these famous giants are right here in our own country. In fact, the tallest tree in the world as well as the biggest tree (largest around) both grow in California.

These two softwood trees belong to the sequoia family. They were named *Sequoia* in honor of the famous Indian chief who worked out the first alphabet for his people.

The tallest tree in the world is a California redwood. It is the *Sequoia sempervirens*. *Sempervirens* means "always green" or "ever living." Both meanings fit it well.

This tree is three hundred sixty-five feet high. It is growing in what is now the Humboldt State Park in Dyerville, California. It is called the Founders Tree, in memory of the founders of the Save-the-Redwoods League. Members of this League worked hard through the years to save this tree, and many other redwoods, from destruction.

All redwoods do not grow quite this tall. The adult trees are usually from two hundred to two hundred seventy-five feet high. Adult redwoods are usually ten to fifteen feet around; exceptional ones sometimes measure nearly twenty feet.

The cones are quite small for such a big tree—no more than an inch long. And they have very few seeds. In fact, some of these small, purplish-brown cones have no seeds at all. And the seeds that do fall find it hard to grow in the thick shade of these big trees.

This might be serious. But the redwood can do something no other evergreen softwood can. It can sprout without seeds. The redwood has no main taproot to go down deep. Instead, thousands of smaller side roots spread out through the ground all around it, and these roots have the power to send up new young trees.

If a redwood is cut down, very soon around the stump a circle of new little trees will spring up from the wide-spreading roots. The stronger trees will live and grow until there is a circle of fine healthy trees around the spot where the old redwood stood.

Sometimes an old redwood tree will crash to the earth. Soon all along its great length of fallen trunk a row of new little trees will sprout and grow, their roots straddling the old log. Come what may, this amazing tree finds some way to send up new shoots, to start life all over. Ever living it surely seems to be!

Redwood needles are as small as the cones—not over an inch long. The needles are flat, sharp-pointed, and a bright olive-green.

The young redwoods are very dainty compared to the full-grown trees. They look somewhat like young hemlocks. The branches droop gracefully and are thick with foliage.

The redwood is fast growing and almost impossible to kill. No insect or disease attacks it. The bark is often a foot thick, which gives protection to the vital parts of the tree. Even fire does not hurt the older redwoods easily. This is because there are plenty of pipelines carrying water up into the tree to keep it moist. Then, too, there is no resin in the tree. Some softwoods are rich in resin, and these woods flame up quickly.

Redwoods live from one thousand to fifteen hundred years. They grow only in a very narrow strip along the California coast, an area about five hundred miles long and twenty or thirty miles wide. They grow far enough inland, however, to be sheltered from the winds, yet close enough to enjoy the wet fog. For this reason, they are also called coast redwoods.

The redwood has played an important part in the history of California. In the early days whole cities were built almost entirely of its fine lumber, and the settlers were wasteful with it.

To keep the redwood forests from being completely cut and destroyed, a Save-the-Redwoods League was formed. Membership in the League, which started with three, has now grown to over fifteen thousand. With money from these citizens, and from the state of California, many fine redwood groves have been bought. These trees are now protected in parks for us and for future generations to enjoy.

In northwestern California you can drive along a highway for miles through forests of redwoods. It's like driving through a quiet cathedral with shafts of sunlight slanting down.

The coast redwood is the tallest tree in the world, but it isn't the largest. The honor of being the largest goes to a big brother of the redwood called the General Sherman tree, which belongs to the *Sequoia gigantea* or "big tree" branch of the family.

This giant is growing in Sequoia National Park in California. It is thirty-six and one-half feet in diameter. Its circumference is nearly one hundred and fifteen feet, and it is two hundred and seventy-two feet tall. There is enough wood in this tree to build thirty-five five-room houses. And there are others almost as big as the General Sherman tree.

The big trees are among the oldest living things in the world. The General Sherman tree, for instance, is over three thousand eight hundred years old. When Columbus discovered America this tree was more than three thousand years old.

The wood of these big trees is very brittle. When the first colonists felled the trees the great trunks

broke when they crashed to the ground, and the huge logs were hard to handle. The lumbermen tried many experiments to cut these trees down so they would not smash. But they finally had to give up and go on to smaller trees that could be felled with less difficulty.

Unfortunately, in their experiments, the men destroyed acre after acre of magnificent groves. Many of these giants were left lying just where they had fallen. Later sheep herders started fires through these groves. They thought fire would make the vegetation grow faster. But it did more harm than good. The fires killed off all the young trees trying to struggle up. The adult big tree can resist fire because of its thick bark and the tannic acid in its sap; but the young, thin-barked tree is easily destroyed.

Finally a group of nature lovers and public-spirited citizens got busy. After a hard fight, and with the aid of such fine men as John Muir and President Theodore Roosevelt, some of the big tree groves were put under the protection of our National Parks. Now, thanks to their efforts, you and many generations to come can see and enjoy these amazing giants of the tree world.

Today there are about seventy separate groves

left. They are scattered along a two hundred and sixty mile area in the California Sierra. The trees grow on the western slopes of the mountains around five thousand to eight thousand feet. This is rugged country. The snow piles up in winter and fierce winds blow. But the trees are tough and seem to thrive on it.

The branches on these old giants start very high, and the great trunks tower up and up like huge columns. The branches are immense, too. If you could stand one of them on the ground it would be taller and bigger around than many another whole tree.

The bright green needles of the big tree are quite different from those of the coast redwood. They lie along the twigs like overlapping scales. The yellowish-brown cones are somewhat larger—one to three inches. But they still look small for such a giant to bear.

Seeds of the big tree sprout more easily than those of the coast redwood. The big tree does not grow in such thick forests, so the seeds fall in sunnier spots. Even so, less than one seed in a million will take root and grow. And, strangely enough, the big trees have to be at least two hundred and fifty years old before they start producing their best seeds.

SEQUOIA GIGANTEA

There are big hardwood trees in our forests, too—not giants, exactly, but towering quite tall. Largest among them is the tulip tree *(Liriodendron tulipifera)*. This grows to two hundred feet and its trunk becomes eight to ten feet thick.

Other common names for this tree are yellow poplar (because of its yellow heartwood), and white poplar or whitewood (because of its white sapwood). Its "tulip tree" name is due to its large white flowers which are shaped very much like a tulip.

You can identify this tree very easily by its leaves. Each leaf has a broad V-shaped notch at the end, as though someone had chopped off the tip! Some people think this notch is shaped like a saddle, and they call it the saddle-leaf tree.

The slender leaf stems twist and turn in the slightest breeze, like those of the aspen. And the tree has a beautiful, shining look as the bright leaves dance in the sunlight. In the fall the leaves turn a clear, bright yellow.

Although the tulip tree belongs to the hardwood family, its wood is softer than any tree in the softwood family except the western white pine and the alpine fir. The wood is very lightweight, too.

Indians and pioneers made many a fine canoe from tulip tree trunks. By hollowing out a single log they could make a light canoe as long as sixty feet. That is why Southerners still call the tulip tree "canoe-wood."

The tulip tree grows in all states east of the Mississippi except Maine and New Hampshire. It grows tallest and best in the southern Appalachians. West of the Mississippi it is found in Louisiana, Arkansas, Oklahoma, and Missouri.

It is one of our most beautiful and valuable hardwoods.

14

OUR SMALLEST TREES

THERE are dwarfs in the tree world, too. The tiniest of them all are found not far from the sequoia giants. These are the pygmy cypress. Some of them are less than one foot high, with a trunk only one-quarter to three-quarters inch thick. But they are sturdy trees and live as long as forty years.

Their botanical name is *Cupressus pygmaea*. Because they grow along the coastal plains in Mendocino County, California, they are sometimes called the Mendocino cypress.

This cypress has a bushy shape. Its bark is thin, reddish brown, and shreddy. The scalelike leaves are dark green and small—not more than one-twelfth of an inch long.

Small as these trees are, they still bear cones, even when they're only six to ten inches tall. The cones are small, too—five to seven-eighths of an inch in diameter—and they take two seasons to ripen.

The trees are small because of the kind of soil in which they grow. This part of the northern California coast is covered with a hard white sandstone. It is called the "white plains" or "barrens." During the rainy season the water does not sink easily into this hardpan. Instead it stands in pools and evaporates later, so during the dry season there is little stored water for the roots to absorb.

Then, too, winds from the ocean whip up the sandstone, swirling it around the trees. Soon every leaf and twig is coated with this cementlike substance. When you see what these trees have to fight against you don't wonder that they're pygmies.

Some pygmy cypress trees are found at higher elevations and in better soil. These grow to be twenty-five to forty feet tall and six to twelve inches around. Even so, they do not seem to be as strong or to live as long as they do when they grow in their native hardpan.

The wood of these small trees is not of much use commercially. They are important, though, because they can grow and hold back the soil in places where other trees could not live at all.

Another of our small trees is the dwarf juniper

(*Juniperus communis*). Unlike the pygmy cypress, this one grows all across the country. It is found in every section of the United States except the extreme southeastern and southwestern sections.

It grows in Canada, too, and in Europe. It is found in more different places than is any other tree in the northern half of the world. For a dwarf it certainly gets around!

Most everywhere this tree grows it is small, usually less than five feet. Only in a few places (in southern Illinois and the mountains of New England, and in the Mediterranean Basin across the sea) does it grow fifteen to twenty-five feet tall.

Even though the wood is not important commercially, the growing tree makes a fine ground cover on waste land and a good windbreak. It holds back the soil, snow masses, and other debris in exposed places where other things cannot grow.

This little tree grows in an unusual way. Often when it is only a sprawling shrub the "stems" or little branches grow out along the ground in the form of a circle. They build up quite high along the edge until the tree begins to look like a large green saucer or bowl. People in England used to say it was where the fairies danced. They called it the "fairy circle."

This juniper, like all other junipers, is an evergreen with "berries" instead of cones. This is what makes it different from similar trees—cedars, for instance. Botanists tell us the berries are really cones with a fleshy covering: the cone scales are there, but they grow too close together for us to see.

The small, round, blue berries are coated with a whitish bloom when ripe. They are fragrant and sweet, and birds love to eat them.

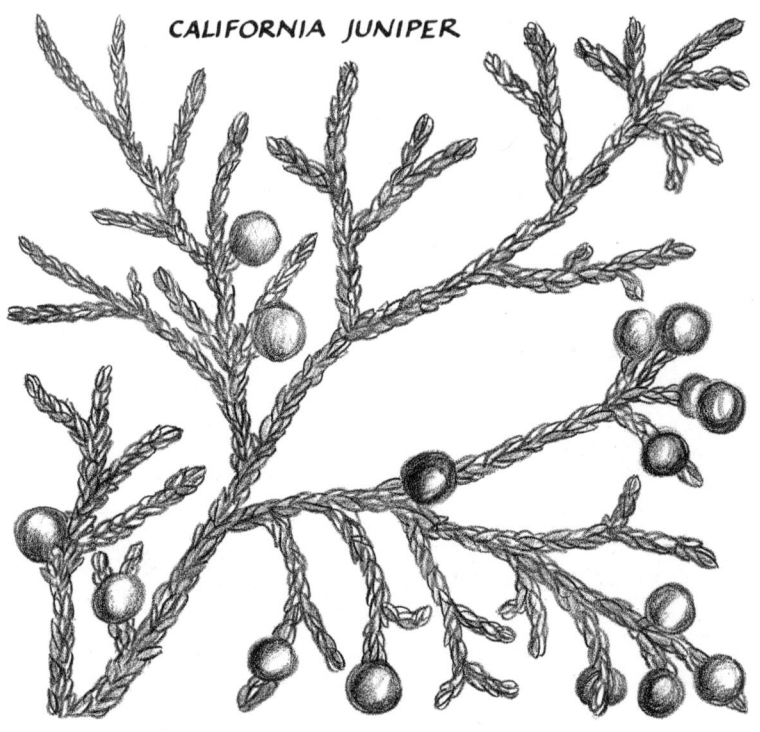
CALIFORNIA JUNIPER

The dwarf juniper differs from other native junipers in its leaves. Where other junipers have scalelike leaves, this tree has needlelike ones.

There are a few small trees among our broadleafs, or hardwoods, too. Two of the smallest are the pussy willow *(Salix discolor)* and the witch hazel *(Hamamelis virginiana)*.

We all know the pussy willow tree, especially for its soft, silky, gray catkin buds that push out on the bare branches in the spring. These willows need

moisture and often are found around swamps and rivers. They grow in the East as far south as Delaware, Indiana, and Illinois, and on to Iowa, Minnesota, and the Black Hills of South Dakota. Often the pussy willow is just shrub size, but sometimes it grows twenty feet tall.

The witch hazel, too, can be a shrub or a tree of twenty feet. There are two things about this tree that are quite unusual. For one thing, the tree flowers in the fall, instead of in the spring. After the leaves have turned yellow and have fallen, tiny yellow blossoms open out and hang down from the branches like crinkly ribbons.

At the same time the long, hairy seed pods, which have been on the tree all year, begin to ripen. Each pod opens wide like a little mouth, and out pop two black seeds, shooting through the air as far as twenty-five to thirty feet.

The wood is hard, but the tree is too small for it to be of much use. However, the popular witch hazel solution sold in drugstores is made from its bark, twigs, and leaves. The witch hazel tree grows from Canada to Florida and west to Minnesota, Iowa, Texas, Louisiana, and Mississippi.

15

OUR RAREST TREES

PROBABLY the rarest tree in America is the Franklin tree. It's a tree you just cannot find—not growing wild, that is.

For over one hundred and fifty years people have been searching for this tree, but without success.

Once, long ago, Franklin trees did grow naturally along the Altamaha River in southeastern Georgia. A Pennsylvania farmer by the name of John Bartram discovered them while on a botanical trip in 1765. He called them Franklin in honor of his good friend, Benjamin Franklin. The botanical name is *Franklinia alatamaha*.

Later John Bartram's son, William, brought back cuttings and seeds of these trees to plant at his Pennsylvania home. Descendants of these trees are there today, and you can visit them at the Bartram Gardens in Philadelphia.

Many new trees have been started from seeds and cuttings of the Bartram trees and sold in nurseries. So today there are quite a few Franklin trees in cultivation. But 1790 is the last record we have of anyone seeing this tree growing wild. What happened to the native trees the Bartrams found? No one seems to know, although botanists have been looking for some sign of these trees ever since. In 1940 the Women's Clubs of Georgia put up a marker near the spot where the trees once grew.

The Franklin tree is one of the loveliest flowering hardwoods. The white blossoms are about three inches across and have gay yellow stamens in the center. In the fall the leaves turn bright crimson.

People who know about these beautiful trees like to plant them in their gardens or yard. You might even have one growing on your own lawn. If you do you can boast that yours is one of the rarest trees in the world.

There are a number of other rare and interesting trees in our country. The big tree sequoia, besides being the biggest, is also one of our rarest trees. So is the little pygmy cypress.

The Santa Lucia fir is another rare tree. *Abies venusta* is its botanical name, and it once grew over quite a wide area. Now there are only a few left. They are making their last stand in a small, thirty-five mile section of the Santa Lucia Mountains in Monterey County, California. There are about one thousand mature trees growing in groups of one hundred or more.

This tree has been called "the most curious fir tree in the world." Nearly everything about it seems strange. For one thing, it grows where there are no other fir trees within a distance of one hundred twenty to two hundred twenty-five miles. The shape of this tree is most unusual, too. Sixty to one hundred feet high, it stretches straight and tall above the pines and hardwoods around it. Toward the top it tapers to a very sharp point. Its height, unusual shape, and dark yellow-green leaves make it very conspicuous. From several miles away you can see it, like a tall green steeple against the sky.

The branches spread quite wide toward the bottom of the tree. They grow thick and low on the trunk; and from them long, slender side branchlets droop gracefully like green tassels. The shining, dark yellow-green leaves are slender with a sharp-pointed tip.

Even the cones are unique. Sticking out from under each cone scale is a sharp-pointed, straw-colored needle, nearly two inches long. The tree is often called the bristlecone fir because of these bristling needles. Often the cones are coated with sticky white pitch, and they glisten in the sun like Christmas tree ornaments.

These trees do not grow easily from seed, which is one reason why they are becoming so rare. Mature trees do not bear cones every year. And when they do, they bear only a few, high up on the tree. Insects and rodents and birds eat many of the seeds from these cones. It isn't easy for men to get these seeds, because most of the trees are growing in wild areas, high on granite walls or rocky ridges.

Some nurserymen have managed to obtain seeds and to grow and sell a few of the trees. They make beautiful ornamentals for the lawn and driveway.

The Santa Lucia firs are in the protection of the National Forest not only because they are so rare but because they make such fine protective covering in dry canyons and over rocky slopes.

Another rare tree is the Monterey cypress *(Cupressus macrocarpa)*. It, too, is found in California, not far from the Santa Lucia fir, the redwoods, and the pygmy cypress.

The Monterey cypress is a sea-loving tree. It clings to the shore, always within a half mile, at least, of the pounding surf. It is native to only two small areas, both near Monterey: Cypress Point and Point Lobos. The total growing space the trees take up in these two areas is probably less than one square mile.

Many of the trees along this winding rocky shore hug the cliffs in spots where no other tree could grow. They bend and bow before the stormy winds that beat against them, but they do not break.

Instead of growing tall they send their matted,

gnarled branches out wide from a leaning, bent trunk. They twist and turn in all sorts of strange shapes. One looks like an octopus, another like a green umbrella. Some, with their grayish-white bark, look like ghosts in the fog that so often swirls about them. No one knows for certain just how old these wild Monterey cypress are. Some authorities think they may be three hundred years or more.

Each year many visitors take the winding drive along the cliffs near Monterey or visit Point Lobos State Park to see these trees. And the pictures that have been taken of them through the years would surely mount up into the millions.

This is the only area in the world where the Monterey cypress grows wild. But thousands of seeds have been gathered from the little grayish-brown cones. They have been planted and grown in other areas away from the seaside cliffs. You can find them on lawns and driveways in different parts of our country. They have been planted as windbreaks on farms and ranches.

They even have been shipped to other parts of the world—Europe, Australia, and New Zealand. Away from the stormy coast they grow tall and handsome, quite as a proper tree should. They do not look at all like the cliff-dweller natives. It is hard

to believe sometimes they are the very same tree. But, for all their protection and care, they do not live as long as the storm-tossed ones along the coast. They thrive for a while, then die, almost as though they were pining for the fog and gales of their native cliffs.

About five hundred miles down the California coast another small group of rare trees sprawl in strange shapes along the hillsides above the sea. These are the Torrey pines *(Pinus torreyana)*. There are only about three thousand of these trees—perhaps the rarest pines in the world.

They grow along a strip about eight miles long and one and one-half miles wide in San Diego County. A few more, perhaps one hundred, can be found on Santa Rosa Island, a bit farther north. But nowhere else in the world do the Torrey pines grow wild.

Whipped by the sea winds, they grow fifteen to twenty feet tall and their limbs sprawl out in every strange shape imaginable. Each tree looks different from the rest. It is as if they are vying with one another to see which can take on the strangest, weirdest form.

Needles of the wild Torrey pine are long—eight to thirteen inches—and grow only in thick clumps at the very ends of the twigs. The cones are huge. They are four to six inches long, nearly as thick, and often weigh as much as one pound.

Seeds in the cones are very sweet, so a great many of them are eaten by birds and rodents. The few seeds that do fall and sprout find it hard to grow in this arid soil along these windswept hillsides. So the trees that have managed to struggle up are protected in this Torrey Pines City Park.

Two rare trees grow in Florida. They are the Florida Torreya and the Florida yew. Nowhere else in the world do they grow wild. And here in Florida they grow in an area that covers only twenty miles in the northwestern part of the state along the eastern bank of the Apalachicola River.

Both these trees belong to the yew family, and they look alike. The best way to tell them apart is by their fruit. The fruit of the Florida Torreya looks rather like an olive or nutmeg. If you crush the needles of this tree you will notice a strong smell. The sap has this smell, too. Because of this the tree has been nicknamed the stinking cedar. But it really isn't that bad.

A western relative of the Torreya, the California nutmeg (it's really a yew) has this same strong smell, and has been given the same nickname. It grows in the California coast ranges and is also quite rare.

Fruit of the Florida yew is small and bright red; it looks like a berry. This tree grows to twenty-five feet while the Florida Torreya reaches fifty feet or more. Both trees are protected now in the Torreya State Park.

16

OUR MOST PLENTIFUL TREES

THE trembling aspen is the only hardwood tree that grows naturally all across the country from sea to sea. You find it from Maine to California and from the Gulf of Mexico almost to the Arctic.

The Indians called this tree "Noisy Leaf," because it seems to be softly rustling most of the time. The leaf stem is soft and flat and flexible as a ribbon. It is set at right angles to the leaf. The tiniest breeze starts each leaf twirling—and sparkling, too. The small, rounded leaves are such a bright, shiny green that they flash in the sunlight like mirrors.

Trembling aspen *(Populus tremuloides)* is one of the prettiest trees in the poplar family. It's rather small—twenty to forty, sometimes sixty, feet tall. It grows best in the sunlight on the edge of the forest. Here its smooth, grayish or greenish-white bark stands out strikingly against the dark of the other forest trees, even in winter.

In spring, the shiny buds open into dangling flowers, or catkins. In autumn the tree seems to blaze in golden glory when the sun strikes its gay yellow leaves.

The trembling aspen grows easily and fast in most any kind of soil and climate. In many places where man has cut or burned the forests away, this aspen has taken over and covered the barren land. Some people have called it a weed tree because it grows so

fast and takes over bare land so easily, and because it does not live very long and its wood is weak and soft.

But most people love it for the beauty and protection it is able to give land that has been spoiled by thoughtless man. And they have found, too, that its wood is valuable as pulp for making paper for magazines.

As the most plentiful of hardwood trees, the oak could boast a bit, too. There are more kinds of oaks in the world than any other tree—over five hundred species. We have about fifty species of oak native to the United States and Canada. About twice as many grow east of the Rockies as west.

There is hardly any part of our country where an oak of some sort does not grow. These trees seem to be able to get along in almost any kind of soil or climate.

Oaks differ in a great many ways—leaves, trunk, size, and habits of growth. One oak even tries to fool us by having leaves so much like a willow you have to look very carefully before you can find it's an oak. But if you know the oak tree's secret you can never be fooled. Look carefully on the tree or on the ground beneath. If you find any sign of an acorn you know the tree is an oak. For every oak in the

world has acorns of some kind. No other tree in the world has this kind of fruit.

Most oaks are deciduous—they drop their leaves in the fall. A few, growing in warmer parts of our country, are evergreen and keep their leaves all year. Like some very friendly people you may know, the oak seems sociable, too. Whenever it grows naturally, you most often find it in groups or groves—seldom alone. The trees are not close together, usually, because the oak needs plenty of room to stretch out its limbs and roots. But others of its kind are seldom far away.

Among the softwoods, the pine is the most plentiful. There are about seventy species of pine, and they are found in many different parts of the world. In fact, pine trees cover a greater area than any other cone-bearing tree. And they are more useful, too, and more important to mankind than any other softwood.

You can always tell a pine from the other softwoods by its needles. They grow in bundles of from two to five. They are long and thin and are fastened together at the base of the bundle by a thin, papery sheath. On all other softwoods the needles are set one by one along the twigs. They never grow in bundles as the pine needles do.

The pine has a very famous history. All down the ages it has played an important part in people's lives. Primitive man used the wood of this tree because it was soft and easy to cut. It floated well, too, and their rafts and small boats were made from pine. This is how the pine tree came by its scientific name of *Pinus*, meaning a raft.

Folk tales of many lands include stories about the pine. The Romans used to eat pine cones to make them strong, thinking they could absorb some of the strength of the tree. And stories are told of thieves and robbers in Bohemia eating the cones for protection. They thought the oil in the nut formed a protective layer under the skin to make them shot-proof.

There's an interesting Greek legend that explains why the pine tree is always green. Cybele, mother of the gods, became angry at a shepherd she loved and turned him into a pine tree. Then she was sorry for what she had done. She sat under the tree day after day, mourning. The Greek god, Jupiter, felt sorry for Cybele. To comfort her he promised her that the pine would always stay green. And it has, to this day.

People of other lands once thought spirits lived in every tree. They thought the holes or knots in the trunk were where the wood spirits escaped into the outer world. And they believed these spirits sometimes turned into real people.

Pine trees have played a very important part in our own country's history. About thirty-five species are native to North America. No matter in what section of the United States you live, you'll probably find some kind of pine growing not far away. It's one of the most plentiful and best-loved trees in our land.

17

THINGS YOU CAN DO

To keep our country green, there are two things every citizen can do:
1. Protect the trees we have.
2. Start new trees and forests.

In order to protect the forests, there are several things that must always be kept in mind. Most people know them, but forget about them. They concern fire and the trees themselves. The following are very important to know and to *remember to do*.

Fire is one of the worst enemies of our forests. Nine out of every ten forest fires are man-made, started by human carelessness. They destroy not only trees and plant life, but animal life, too. *Never* start a fire in or near the woods on a windy day. When you do build a fire, be sure it is built in a

THINGS YOU CAN DO

wide, cleared space. Or clear a space yourself for several feet around.

After lighting a match, break it in two so you will be *sure* it is out. Before you leave, put your fire *out* with water. Then shovel earth well over the ashes.

Never hurt the bark on trees. Remember that trees need their bark for protection, just as we need our skin. Don't trample or chop roots of trees. Don't trample or cut down small saplings. These are big trees in the making.

There is great satisfaction in starting new trees, perhaps even a new forest. Watching tree seeds or seedlings grow into trees takes patience and time, but it is worth the waiting.

Seeds of some of the hardwoods—the elm, willow, and cottonwood—ripen in spring or early summer. Seeds of this kind should be planted as soon as you gather them, before they dry out.

In fact, spring is the time to plant any tree seeds. However, quite a few tree seeds ripen in late summer or early fall. Seeds from softwoods, for example, ripen then and should be collected as soon as the cones are ripe—from September to November. For as soon as the cone scales open, the seeds fly away on the wind. If you watch where the squirrels are cutting the cones you probably can get one of the ripe cones they drop and take your seeds from it.

In the fall you can gather seeds from some of the hardwoods, too—trees such as the walnut, buckeye, laurel, and many of the oaks. You will find their seeds in the nuts, pods, or acorns on the ground under the trees.

Many tree seeds dry out quickly. Since they cannot be planted until spring, fall seeds will have to be stored carefully until then. The best way to store seeds collected in the fall is to place them in a tight metal or glass container. Keep them in a cool, dark place in the basement or in a refrigerator where the temperature is around forty degrees.

In the spring you can plant the larger tree seeds—acorns, hickory nuts, and walnuts—right in the garden. Plant them two or three inches apart and cover lightly with about one-half inch of dirt. Keep them well watered. It is well to place a screen or fine chicken wire over the beds to protect the new seedlings from birds. You can remove this when the seedlings are two or four inches tall. And when they are about ten inches tall, transplant them to places where they are to grow.

The smaller seeds can be planted in a small nursery flat or shallow box. Put in some good sandy loam

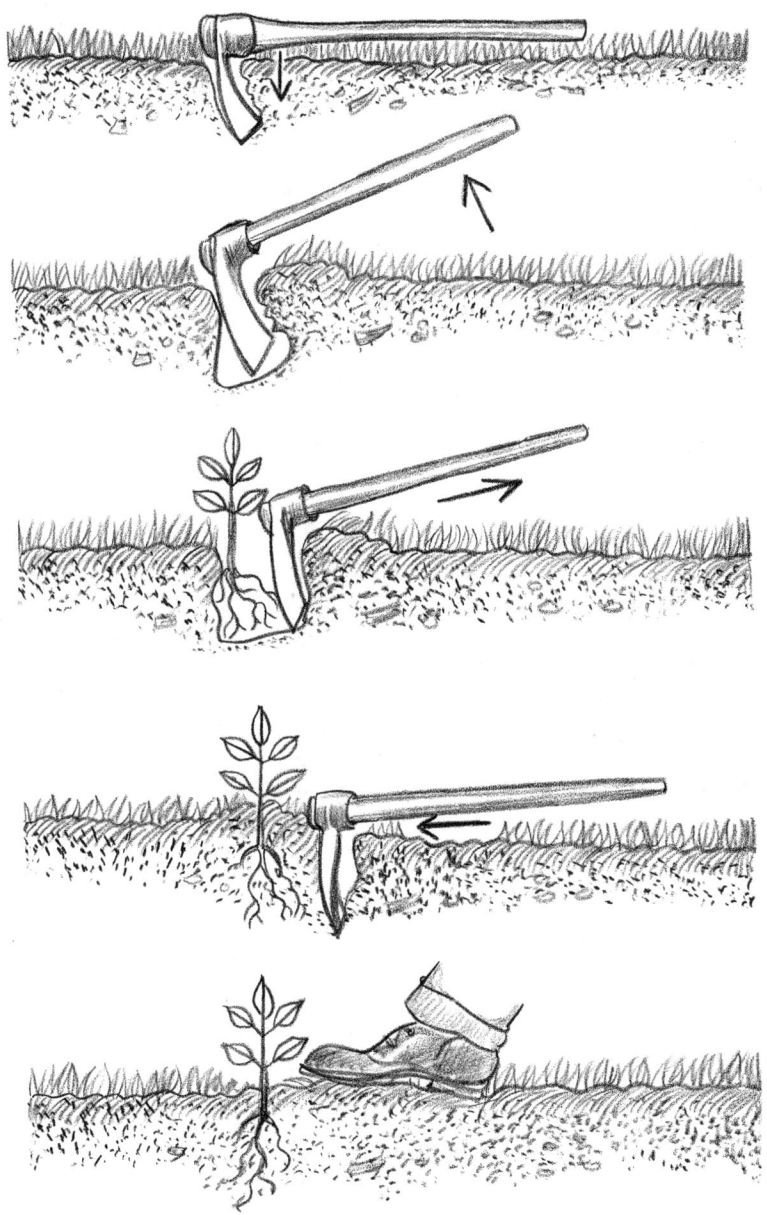

and scatter the seeds. Then press the seeds, just slightly, into the soil and cover them lightly with sand or soil.

Keep the boxes in the shade and water carefully with a light spray. It's a good idea to place a screen over the flat to keep out the birds.

You can transplant the trees from the boxes when they are two to four inches tall. Put them in individual pots or gallon cans, and keep them there until they are eight or ten inches tall. Then you can set them out where they are to grow. Be sure to keep all seedlings well watered and well weeded.

Some trees, such as the willow and the cottonwood, can be started from twigs. Just break off a twig from one of the trees. Stick it into some good soil, about half its length. Keep it watered and weeded, and before long it will start growing, putting out new leaves and shoots.

Perhaps you would like to have a hand in starting a whole new forest. Our Forest Service tells us there are more than sixty million acres of forest land that need planting in the United States! Here is a chance to do a fine, patriotic thing.

See if there is any land nearby that is not being used. This may be just the place to grow a fine crop of trees. Try to get your parents and friends to help

THINGS YOU CAN DO

you. Or, better still, perhaps you can start a school project. Often school groups can get permission to take over some piece of unused land in the town.

Trees can be planted on any idle land, even on land that has been ruined by erosion, or in rocky, hilly places. Anything from one to twenty acres can be turned into a reforesting project.

Since raising trees from seed is rather slow, you may prefer to plant your new forest with little trees which have already been started.

Almost every state, in its State Nursery, raises trees to be used for planting idle forest lands. You can buy small seedlings from them for about two cents each. Some private growers or nurseries will furnish small trees at around five cents each.

You might write your State Forester for information and help. Ask him how you would go about getting seedlings to plant in your school forest or in other land. He will suggest the best trees to plant in your particular part of the country, too, and perhaps send along some instructions for planting and caring for your new forest. The following suggestions may help:

The best time to plant the seedlings will vary in different parts of the country. Generally, springtime planting is best, when the weather is favorable and the ground ready to work easily. Seedlings stand a better chance of living if the weather is not extremely hot or extremely cold or the ground very dry or very wet.

Some seedlings come in tar-paper pots packed fifty to a flat. Always prepare the planting holes in the ground before removing the seedlings from the flat. Dig each hole deeply enough for the roots to be well covered, but not so deep as to cover leaves or twigs.

When removing seedlings from the flat some of the tar paper may come off, but try not to disturb the ball of soil around the roots. Never let the seedlings dry out. Place each in its prepared hole, pack soil around it carefully but firmly, and water well.

If you are planting larger, bare-root seedlings, dig a round hole, large enough around so the roots will not be crowded and about a foot deeper than the tree roots. Put a three- or four-inch layer of fertilizer in the bottom of the hole. Then place a layer of topsoil over this, making sure the fertilizer is well covered so the roots will not touch it. Shape the topsoil into a mound in the center and carefully spread the roots out over it. Then fill in with earth and water well. Keep all seedlings weeded—and watered, if the weather is dry—until they are well established.

THINGS YOU CAN DO

The list at the end of this chapter will tell you where to write to your State Forester.

You might ask if there is a 4-H Club near you that is carrying on forestry and conservation projects. If there is, join it and work with them. You will find it a wonderful experience. Good luck and good "foresting!"

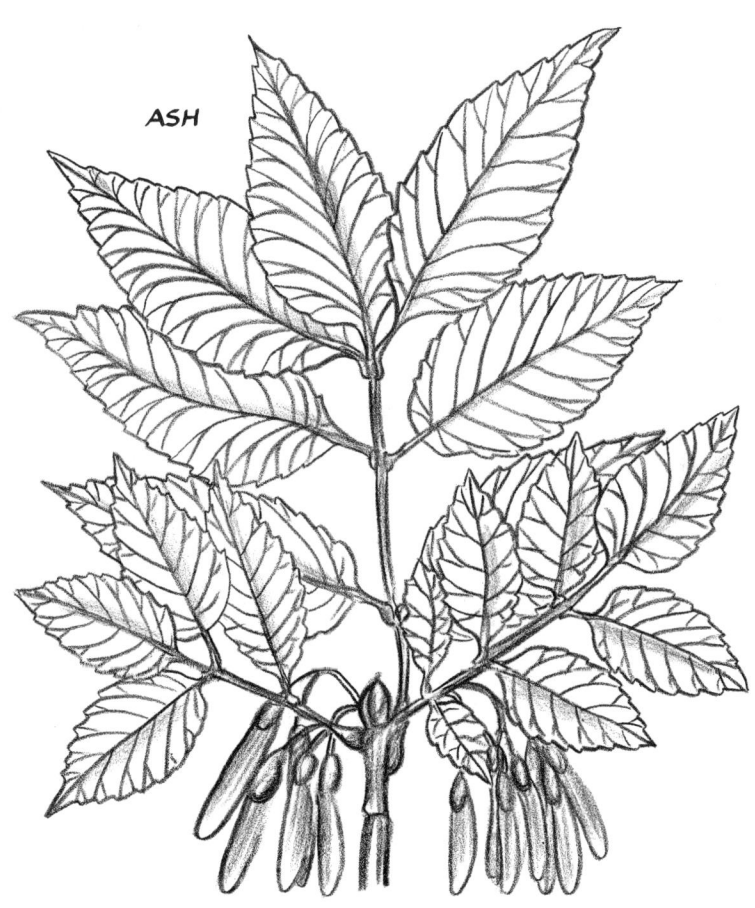

ASH

Alabama	State Forester, 5 N. Bainbridge Street, Montgomery 4.
Arizona	None.
Arkansas	Forest Director, P.O. Box 1940, Little Rock.
California	State Forester, State Office Bldg. #1, Sacramento 14.
Colorado	Ext. Forester, Colorado A.&M. College, Port Collins.
Connecticut	State Forester, 165 Capitol Avenue, Hartford 15.
Delaware	State Forester, State House, Dover.
Florida	State Forester, P.O. Box 1200, Tallahassee.
Georgia	Forest Director, State Capitol, Atlanta 3.
Hawaii	Terr. Forester, P.O. Box 5425, Pawaa Substation, Honolulu.
Idaho	Dean of Forestry, University of Idaho, Moscow.
Illinois	State Forester, 301½ E. Monroe Street, Springfield.
Indiana	State Forester, 311-325 W. Washington Street, Indianapolis 9.
Iowa	Supt. of Forests, 7th & Court Streets, Des Moines 9.
Kansas	Ext. Forester, State College, Manhattan.
Kentucky	Forester Director, Division of Forestry, Frankfort.
Louisiana	State Forester, P.O. Box 1269, Baton Rouge 1.
Maine	State Forester, Maine Forest Service, Augusta.

Maryland	Forest Director, State Office Bldg., Annapolis.
Massachusetts	Forest Director, 15 Ashburton Place, Boston 8.
Michigan	Dir. Div. of Conservation, Michigan State College, East Lansing.
Minnesota	Forest Director, State Office Bldg., St. Paul 1.
Mississippi	State Forester, P.O. Box 649, Jackson 5.
Missouri	State Forester, Jefferson City.
Montana	Dean of Forestry, Montana State University, Missoula.
Nebraska	Ext. Forester, University of Nebraska, Lincoln 1.
Nevada	Ext. Forester, State Capitol, Carson City.
New Hampshire	State Forester, State Office Bldg., Concord.
New Jersey	State Forester, State House Annex, Trenton 7.
New Mexico	None.
New York	Forest Director, Lands & Forests Div., Albany 7.
North Carolina	State Forester, P.O. Box 2719, Raleigh.
North Dakota	State Forester, Bottineau.
Ohio	Chief, Forestry, 1500 Dublin Road, Columbus.
Oklahoma	Forest Director, 536 State Capitol, Oklahoma City 5.
Oregon	State Forester, Salem.
Pennsylvania	Chief, Forests, Bureau of Forests, Harrisburg.

Rhode Island	Chief Forester, 18 State House, Providence 2.
South Carolina	State Forester, 506 Calhoun Office Bldg., Columbia 1.
South Dakota	State Forester, Pierre.
Tennessee	State Forester, 309 New State Office Bldg., Nashville 3.
Texas	Forest Director, A.&M. College, College Station 5.
Utah	Forestry Professor, Utah State Agricultural College, Logan.
Vermont	State Forester, Montpelier.
Virginia	State Forester, University Station, Charlottesville.
Washington	Forestry Head, State College of Washington, Pullman.
West Virginia	State Forester, Charleston 5.
Wisconsin	Conservation Director, Madison 2.
Wyoming	Asst. Director, Experiment Station, Laramie.

List from the Government bulletin, *How Man Starts New Forests*, United States Department of Agriculture, Forest Service. Washington, D. C.

BOOKS ABOUT TREES

Cater, Ruth Cooley. *Tree Trails and Hobbies.* New York: Doubleday and Company, Inc., 1950.

Collis, John Stewart. *The Triumph of the Tree.* New York: William Sloane Associates, Inc., 1954.

Cormack, Maribelle. *The First Book of Trees.* New York: Franklin Watts, Inc., 1951.

Cosgrove, Margaret. *Wonders of the Tree World.* New York: Dodd, Mead and Company, 1953.

Emerson, Arthur I., and Weed, Clarence M. *Our Trees: How to Know Them.* Garden City, New York: Garden City Books.

Greeley, William B. *Forests and Men.* New York: Doubleday and Company, Inc., 1951.

Hylander, Clarence J. *Trees and Trails.* New York: The Macmillan Company, 1952.

Kieran, John. *An Introduction to Trees.* Garden City, New York: Hanover House, 1954.

Lane, Dr. Ferdinand C. *The Story of Trees.* New York: Doubleday and Company, Inc., 1952.

Lillard, Richard G. *The Great Forest.* New York: Alfred A. Knopf, Inc., 1947.

McKenny, Margaret. *Trees of the Countryside.* New York: Alfred A. Knopf, Inc., 1942.

Peattie, Donald Culross. *A Natural History of Trees of Eastern and Central North America.* Boston: Houghton Mifflin Company, 1950.

Peattie, Donald Culross. *A Natural History of Western Trees*. Boston: Houghton Mifflin Company, 1952.

Platt, Rutherford. *American Trees, A Book of Discovery*. New York: Dodd, Mead and Company, 1952.

Selsam, Millicent E. *Play with Trees*. New York: William Morrow and Company, Inc., 1950.

Sterling, Dorothy. *Trees And Their Story*. New York: Doubleday and Company, Inc., 1953.

Webber, Irma E. *Thanks to Trees*. New York: William R. Scott, Inc., 1952.

INDEX

Abies venusta, 117
Acer saccharum, 57
acorns, 63, 64, 65, 127-128
adhesives, 88
age, determination of:
    maple, 60
    Monterey cypress, 20
    oak, 63
    redwood, 100-101
    softwoods, 51-52
alcohol, 73
America, colonial, 1-5
American Forestry Association, 46
Appalachian Mountains, 32
apple, 95-96
Appleseed, Johnny, 96
ash, 32, 34, 57, 69, 77
aspen, 30, 72
aspen, trembling, 124-126
autumn color changes, 61

balance in nature, 26
bald cypress, 38
balsam, 30, 76
balsa resin, 88
bark, 19, 21, 131
Bartram, John and William, 115
Bartram Gardens, 115-116
basswood, 72, 92
beech, 32, 69, 77
beechnut, 91

beefwood, 38
beetle, locust, 70
beverages, 92
bibliography, 141-142
birch, 22, 30, 32, 57, 69, 77, 92
Black Hills, 44
Black Hills spruce, 78-79
black locust, 69-70
black walnut, 32
blight, chestnut, 85
Bohemia, 128-129
bract, 50
broadleaf trees, 28-29
briquets, 68

cabins, log, 4
California nutmeg tree, 123
California redwoods, 97-104
cambium layer, 19, 21
campgrounds, public, 44
Canadian pulp forests, 79
canoewood, 107
carbohydrates, 14
carbon dioxide, 14
Carya illinoensis, 93
cedar, 72
cellophane, 31, 82
cellulose, 76, 81
Chardonnet, Hilaire de, Count, 80
Charter Oak, 67
chemicals, from wood, 84-89

cherry, 69, 91
chestnut, 85, 77
chestnut blight, 85
chewing gum, 88
China, 73, 84
chinquapin, 91
chlorophyll, 13
chloroplast, 13
chokecherry, 91
CCC (Civilian Conservation Corps), 43
climate, effect of trees upon, 23-26
cloth from wood, 80-83
coffee, 92
Columbus, 101
conifers, 28, 29
conservation, 5, 8-9, 131
consumption of fuel wood, 68, 73
consumption of paper, 79
crab apple, 91, 95
Crete, 73
crops, trees as, 45-47
Cupressus macrocarpa, 119
Cupressus pygmaea, 108
cutting, tree, 6, 33, 45-46
Cybele, 129
cypress, 32, 72
cypress, bald, 38
cypress, pygmy, 108-109

deciduous forests, 32-33
deciduous trees, 29
Department of Agriculture, 43
depression in America, 43
Digger pine, 88
Douglas fir, 37, 49-51, 92
drugs, 88
dwarf juniper, 109-111
dwarf trees, 108-114

edible buds, 92
education, forestry, 47
Egypt, 84
elderberry, 91
elm, 32, 69, 77
Englemann's spruce, 34
erosion, 25-26, 135
eucalyptus, 69
evergreen trees, 29
export, lumber, 5-6
extracts, flavoring, 88

fairies, 110
farms, tree, 45-47
filbert, 91
fir, 30, 76
   Douglas, 37, 49-51, 92
fire, forest, 6, 8-9, 130-131
fire trails and roadways, 43
flavorings, 88, 92
floods, 8, 25, 26
Florida Torreya tree, 123
Florida yew, 123
food-bearing trees, 90-96
food, storage of, by trees, 16
Forest Service, 8-9, 31, 42, 44-46, 134
Founders Tree, 98
4-H Club, 137
Franklin, Benjamin, 115
Franklinia alatamaha, 115
Franklin tree, 115-117
fruit trees, 90-91
fuel trees, 30, 68-73
furniture wood, 57

General Sherman tree, 101
girdling, tree, 3
grafting, 96
Great Britain, 4-5
Great Lakes, 30, 44
Great Plains, 1

INDEX

Greece, 73
growth, tree, 10-22
gum, sweet, 32, 34, 57, 77, 88

Hamamelis virginiana, 112
hardpan, 109
hardwoods, 22, 29, 32, 34, 38, 57, 77
Harrison, Benjamin, President, 43
heartwood, 19, 21
helicopter, in reforestation, 46
hemlock, 30, 31, 85, 92
    western, 76, 81-83
heptane, 88
hickory, 22, 32, 69, 71-72, 90, 91
history, trees in, 67, 128-129
holly, 92
Humbolt State Park, 97

Idaho forest fire of 1910, 8-9
Indians, 58-59, 72, 97, 107, 124

Jackson, Andrew, General, 71-72
Jefferson, Thomas, President, 95
Jeffrey pine, 88
juniper, dwarf, 109-111
Juniperus communis, 110
Jupiter, 129

larch, 30
largest tree, 101
laws, forestry, 47
leaf surface, 15
leaves, 12-13
leaves, oak, 64
legends, 65, 110, 128-129
linden, 32
Liquidambar styraciflua, 88
Liriodendron tulipifera, 105
live oak, 38

loblolly pine, 53
locust, black, 69-70
lodgepole pine, 34
longleaf pine, 53
lumber, 34
lumber companies, 45
lumber trees, 48-56, 57-67

magnolia, 32
mahogany, 38
mangrove, 38
maple tree, sugar, 30, 32, 57-60, 69, 77
masts, ship, 4
matches, 131
Mississippi Valley, 1
Monterey cypress, 119-121
mosquito control, 26
Mount Vernon, 95
Muir, John, 103
mulberry, 91

National Forests, 42-44
naval stores, 85-87
navy, British, 4
New England, 4, 7, 30
newspapers, 79
nut trees, 72, 90-91

oak, 32, 34, 38, 57, 61-64, 69, 77, 126-127
oil, 15
"Old Hickory," 71
oleoresin, 86-87
orange, 90
orchard trees, 90, 95-96
Oregon white oak, 63-64
ownership of forests, 44-45
oxygen exchange, 14, 23

Pacific northwest, 50
paint, 85

palm, 27, 37, 38, 92
paper, 74-79
papyrus, 74
patents, 96
pawpaw, 91
peach, 90
pecan, 90, 91, 92-95
perfume, 88
persimmon, 91
"Peshtigo Horror," 6
photosynthesis, 12
Picea glauca, 77
Picea glauca albertiana, 78-79
Pilgrims, 1-2, 95
pinyon, 91
pioneers, 45-46, 91-92, 93, 107
pines, 51, 88, 128-129
 Southern yellow, 33, 52-55
 white, 4-6, 7, 31, 33, 36, 56
Pinus, 128
Pinus caribaea, 54-55
Pinus echinata, 54
Pinus palustris, 55
Pinus ponderosa, 51
Pinus taeda, 55-56
Pinus torreyana, 122
pitch, 85
planting, tree, 135-136
plastics, 31, 81
plum, 90, 91
Point Lobos State Park, 120
poplar, 72, 76
Populus tremuloides, 124
production of hardwood, 57
production of softwood, 52
products, wood, 31, 48, 58, 73, 79, 80, 81, 85, 88, 89
protection of trees, 130-131
proteins, 15
Pseudotsuga taxifolia, 49
pulp companies, 45
pulpwood, 30, 34, 76, 126

pussy willow, 112-113
pygmy cypress, 108-109

Quercus, 61
Quercus alba, 62
Quercus borealis, 64
Quercus garryana, 63-64

rafts, pine, 128
ranger stations, 43
rare trees, 115-123
rayon, 31, 81
Reaumur, 75
redbud, 92
red oak, 64
red pine, 31
redwood, 37, 72
redwood, California, 97-104
reforestation, 36, 43-44, 46-47, 135
resin, 54, 72, 87-88
rings, in tree age, 21
Robinia pseudoacacia, 69
Rocky Mountains, 2, 34, 36
Romans, 128
Roosevelt, Franklin D., President, 43
Roosevelt, Theodore, President, 42-43, 103
roots, 16-19, 26
rosin, 34, 86-89

Salix discolor, 112
Santa Lucia fir, 117-119
Santa Rosa Island, 122
sapwood, 19
sassafras, 92
Save-the-Redwoods League, 98, 100
sawmills, 4, 5-6
seedling trees, culture of, 132-136

INDEX

seeds, maple, 61
Sequoia, 97
Sequoia gigantea, 101
Sequoia National Park, 101
Sequoia semper virens, 97
serviceberry, 91
shagbark, 22
"shelter belt," 44
shelter, wind, 26
shortleaf pine, 53
silkworms, 80
smallest trees, 108-114
slash pine, 53-55
softwood trees, 27, 29, 34, 37, 53-55, 76-77
spruce, 30, 37, 72, 76, 78-79
starch, 15-16
State Foresters, 135, 138-140
State Nursery, 135
stomata, 14, 23
storax, 88
structure, tree, 10-22
sugar, tree, 14-16
sumac, 92
sunlight, in tree growth, 12-13
swamps, 26, 54-55, 113
swamp bay, 92
sweet gum, 32, 34, 57, 77, 88
sycamore, 22

tallest tree, 97
tannin, 84-85
tar, 85
Torreya State Park, 123

Torrey pines, 122-123
tropical trees, 38
trunk, tree, 19, 21-22
Tsuga heterophylla, 81
tupelo, 39, 77
tulip tree, 32, 105, 107
turpentine, 34, 54, 86-87

vapor, tree, 23-24
varnish, 86
virgin forest, 37

Wadsworth Oak, 67
walnut, 57, 90, 91
walnut, black, 32
Washington, George, President, 95
waste wood, uses of, 68
water absorption, 25
water evaporation, 23-24
weed trees, 30-31, 125-126
western hemlock, 76, 81-83
western white pine, 36
white oak, 62
white pine, 4-6, 7, 31, 33, 56
white spruce, 77
willow, 23, 77
willow, pussy, 112-113
wind, 24, 29, 46, 130
windbreak, 44, 110, 120
witch hazel, 112-114
WPA (Works Progress Administration), 44

About the Author

Miss Dudley's home in Pacific Palisades, California, is not far from several beautiful forest areas, and going there to study trees is an easy matter for her. But trees are just one of Miss Dudley's many interests. Her long list of hobbies includes hiking and camping, sea shells, ceramics, flora and fauna of the desert, mountains and seashore, birds, cats, photography, and her nieces and nephews!

Miss Dudley was born and spent most of her childhood in northern New York state. After graduation from the Medill School of Journalism, Northwestern University, and some graduate study in psychology at Columbia, she began a series of occupations as interesting and varied as her hobbies. In the past she had done sales work in New York, been a society editor of a suburban newspaper, carried out a sales promotion program in a mail order house, worked in a bakery, and even worked on the graveyard shift in a defense plant during the war. She is at present a free-lance writer and photographer.

Articles and photo stories by Miss Dudley have appeared in such magazines as *Nature, Natural History, Child Life,* and *Country Gentleman.*